CONTENTS

Introduction

Crime and Justice is the seventh volume in the series: **Issues For The Nineties**. The aim of this series is to offer up-to-date information about important issues in our world.

Crime and Justice looks at the rising crime rate, especially among the young, crime prevention and the debate about the re-introduction of the death penalty. The information comes from a wide variety of sources and includes:

Government reports and statistics
Newspaper reports and features
Magazine articles and surveys
Literature from lobby groups
and charitable organisations.

It is hoped that, as you read about the many aspects of the issues explored in this book, you will critically evaluate the information presented. It is important that you decide whether you are being presented with facts or opinions. Does the writer give a biased or an unbiased report? If an opinion is being expressed, do you agree with the writer?

Crime and Justice offers a useful starting point for those who need convenient access to information about the many issues involved. However, it is only a starting point. At the back of the book is a list of organisations which you may want to contact for further information.

*****

Killings rise as Britain becomes more violent

Latest crime figures show people are more at risk while property is safe and highlight differences in policing across the country

By Heather Mills
Home Affairs Correspondent

Britain is becoming a more violent place to live in, according to the latest crime figures recorded by the police.

Despite property crime continuing its downward trend, murder, rape, robbery and mugging are all on the increase. There were 331,500 violent crimes recorded in 1994, a 6 per cent rise on the previous year. In particular, the number of killings, which has remained around the 650 mark for about 14 years, has suddenly increased by 9 per cent to 727.

But yesterday David Maclean, the Home Office minister, stressed that crimes of violence still only accounted for 6 per cent of all the 5,251,100 offences recorded last year in England and Wales. He hailed the overall 5 per cent drop in crimes as a 'testament to the hard work done by the police'. The figures represented the largest percentage fall over a two-year period for more than 40 years, he said.

The figures were released as Michael Howard, the Home Secretary, began a nationwide tour aimed at recapturing the law-and-order initiative. But Labour at once seized on the increase in violence to attack Mr Howard's plans to introduce a cheaper scheme of victim compensation. Accused by the Law Lords of unlawful abuse of power last week, Mr Howard says he will introduce new legislation to force through his fixed-rate compensation scheme.

Yesterday, Jack Straw, Labour's home affairs spokesman, said: 'The Government has made victims pay for its failure to stem the rise of violent crime. Instead of cutting violent crime, they have sought to cut the help available for victims.'

Adding to ministers' concerns were the indications yesterday that the downward trend of the last two years appeared to have bottomed out. The drop in recorded crime for the last quarter of 1994 has slowed down to just 1 per cent.

But privately ministers and the opposition spokesman acknowledge that recorded figures are unreliable, giving just a glimpse of the true picture.

The real crime figures are not known because most go unreported. Research for the British Crime Survey tries to get close to the real figure by detailed questioning of 14,500 households – and it shows a slow but continuing increase running at about three times the level of the recorded figures.

Yesterday, 38 of the 43 police forces reported fewer crimes in 1994 than in the previous year. The greatest fall was 10 per cent in vehicle crime – the biggest for 40 years. Burglary was down 8 per cent to 1.3 million and theft down 7 per cent to 2.6 million.

However, rapes rose by 11 per cent to 5,100, robberies increased by 3 per cent to 59,800 and life-threatening attacks rose by 12,700, or 7 per cent.

The general trend appears to support Home Office research showing that crimes of violence increase when the economy improves, while property crime rises during periods of recession and high unemployment.

© The Independent
April, 1995

Car and property crime falls as violence rises

Alan Travis on the disputed reasons for improved figures on theft and burglary

The 10 per cent fall in car crime, the largest for 40 years, during 1994 and the 300,000 reduction in the number of burglaries and other property crimes is attributed by Home Office ministers to increased targeting by the police and better crime prevention.

But criminologists continue to insist that the fall in property crime and the rise in violent offences is linked to the state of the economy.

Home Office researchers yesterday pointed out that the latest crime statistics confirmed for the fifth year running an official study published in 1990 which showed that 'during periods or rapid consumption growth, the increase in property crime tended to slow, while that of personal crime tended to quicken.'

The dramatic falls in property crime recorded yesterday have coincided with police campaigns around the country targeting repeat burglars and with an increase in the level of crime prevention devices fitted to cars. British cars now have a higher standard of locks and alarms than most others in Europe.

> *Criminologists continue to insist that the fall in property crime and the rise in violent offences is linked to the state of the economy*

For the first time in seven years, the official figures recorded an actual fall in the number of burglaries, down 112,000 to 1.3 million. For the second year running there was a fall in thefts, including handling stolen goods, which was down 193,000 offences to 2.6 million crimes. The statistics show that the falls in property crime were experienced in most police force areas.

Overall, violent crime increased by 17,300 offences or 6 per cent. Within this, the increase in violence against the person of 14,200 offences or 7 per cent was made up of 1,500 more life threatening offences and 12,700 less serious offences, including street attacks such as actual bodily harm. The statistics show that two thirds of violent crime was cleared up in 1994.

The murder rate, which is usually remarkably steady in England and Wales, rose sharply from 670 homicides in 1993 to 727 in 1994 but this was partly accounted for by the discovery of the bodies in the Gloucester murder case and the sex cinema fire in London which claimed 11 lives. They also reported an 11 per cent increase in the number of recorded rapes which rose 493 to 5,082, some of which ministers attributed to an increased willingness among victims to go to the police.

Sir Paul Condon, the Metropolitan police commissioner, said yesterday that he now intended targeting criminals involved in street robbery. He stressed that while its aim would be to stop the upward trend in such attacks more than 75 per cent of victims were under the age of 40.

He claimed some of the increase in violent crime was a result of a harder line on domestic violence attackers: 'We now lean towards arresting rather than not arresting,

British Crime Survey

The *British Crime Survey* (BCS) asks adult members of the public, 14,500 in the latest survey, about their experience as a victim of crime in the last year. It's a better guide to victims' experience of crime but it, too, has problems. People may forget some incidents, or not want to disclose crimes they have not reported to the police.

The *British Crime Survey* estimates that, in total, the number of crimes actually committed is nearly four times the number recorded by the police.

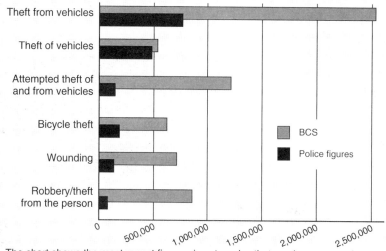

The chart shows the most recent figures, in categories that can be compared, for crimes that took place in England and Wales during 1993.

with charging rather than cautioning, and keeping offenders in custody, rather than releasing them on bail,' said Sir Paul.

'We decided to record any crime of violence as being a crime that had been committed, even if the victim later decided not to proceed with the complaint. This accounted for about two thirds of the increase in violent crime in London,' said Sir Paul. Racial attacks were also believed to have increased by 20 per cent.

The official statistics published yesterday show the fall in crime was spread evenly throughout the country. Thirty-eight of the 43 police forces recorded reductions with the largest falls taking place in Norfolk, Dyfed-Powys, Bedfordshire and Surrey. The five forces which saw increases in crime were North Yorkshire, Dorset, West Mercia, Gloucestershire and Cleveland.

© *The Guardian*
April, 1995

Crimes solved

	per officer		per officer
Nottinghamshire	14.0	North Wales	9.6
Lincolnshire	13.9	South Wales	9.6
Gwent	13.8	Cumbria	9.5
Cleveland	12.7	Dyfed/Powys	9.3
Northamptonshire	12.5	Devon/Cornwall	9.2
Durham	11.4	Lancashire	9.2
Wiltshire	11.4	Derbyshire	9.1
Kent	11.0	Essex	9.0
Dorset	10.8	Thames Valley	9.0
Cambridgeshire	10.6	Avon/Somerset	8.7
Norfolk	10.5	West Mercia	8.7
Humberside	10.4	South Yorkshire	8.6
North Yorkshire	10.4	Warwickshire	8.1
Northumbria	10.2	Bedfordshire	8.0
Gloucestershire	9.9	Greater Manchester	8.0
Hampshire/IOW	9.9	Sussex	7.8
Cheshire	9.9	West Midlands	7.8
West Yorkshire	9.8	Merseyside	7.3
Staffordshire	9.8	Surrey	6.8
Leicestershire	9.7	Hertfordshire	6.5
Suffolk	9.6	Metropolitan Police	5.5

Source: Audit Commission

Rising and falling crime rates

Percentage change 1993-1994

- All offences
- Theft from vehicle
- Theft of vehicle
- Theft from shop
- Theft from person
- Theft of pedal cycle
- Other theft/handling
- Burglary in dwelling
- Burglary other
- Criminal damage
- Fraud and forgery
- Violence against person
- Sexual offences
- Robbery
- Other offences

−12 −8 −4 0 4 8 12 16 20

© *Home Office*
April, 1995

Violent crime, 1994

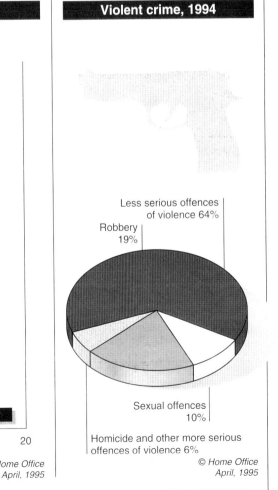

Less serious offences of violence 64%

Robbery 19%

Sexual offences 10%

Homicide and other more serious offences of violence 6%

© *Home Office*
April, 1995

Children and crime

From The Howard League for Penal Reform

The earliest age which children can be brought to a court for criminal proceedings is 10 years. Below this age a child cannot be found guilty of a criminal offence.

Until recently a child between the ages of 10 and 13 years charged with an offence was presumed not to be able to understand what they had done was wrong. For a child of this age to be found guilty, the prosecution had to satisfy the court that the child committed the offence and that they knew what they were doing was seriously wrong. This legal concept is known as *doli incapax*. In March 1994 this presumption was abolished by the Divisional Court in London (Curry v. Director of Public Prosecutions). The case has now been taken to the House of Lords on appeal.

The Sexual Offences Act 1993 abolishes the presumption that boys under 14 years are incapable of offences involving sexual intercourse. The abolition of these two presumptions represents an attack on the age limit at which children are deemed criminally responsible.

The Department of Health has responsibility for the majority of children's legislation. Local authority social service departments have major responsibilities for children who commit or allegedly commit crimes and act under the direction of the Secretary of State for Health.

In 1985 the number of known offenders aged 10-13 peaked at 51,000 for boys and 13,900 for girls. Since then there has been a sharp fall and by 1992 the number of known male offenders fell to 30,900, a fall of 40%. The number of known female offenders fell to 9,100, a fall of 35%. This fall cannot be explained by demographic factors as the population in this age group did not change between 1985 and 1991.

A majority, 57%, of children are cautioned or found guilty of theft

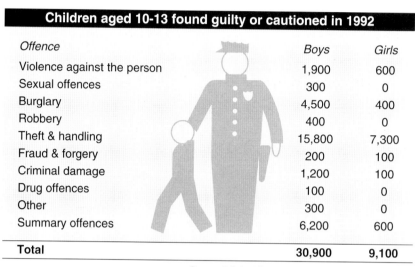

Children aged 10-13 found guilty or cautioned in 1992		
Offence	Boys	Girls
Violence against the person	1,900	600
Sexual offences	300	0
Burglary	4,500	400
Robbery	400	0
Theft & handling	15,800	7,300
Fraud & forgery	200	100
Criminal damage	1,200	100
Drug offences	100	0
Other	300	0
Summary offences	6,200	600
Total	**30,900**	**9,100**

Source: Criminal Statistics England and Wales 1992

or handling, while 6% are cautioned or found guilty of violent offences.

A vast majority of children are dealt with by using a police caution. The caution is a quick response to children's wrongdoing. The involvement of the police is often sufficient to bring home the seriousness of their wrong-doing without the alienating and stigmatising court experience. In some circumstances children may admit their guilt even if they have a legitimate defence.

Most children under 18 years are brought before specially constituted magistrates' courts known as youth courts

---

In 1992, 94% of known offenders ages 10-13 years were cautioned. Home Office research (1985) found that 89% of children under 14 who were cautioned were not convicted of a further offence within 2 years.

The Bail Act 1976 applies to juveniles in the same way as it applies to adults. There is a presumption that bail will be granted unless the court

believes that the defendant will fail to surrender to custody, commit an offence while on bail, interfere with a witness or obstruct the course of justice. Additionally, children who are under 17 years may be refused bail by the court for their own welfare.

Young people who are refused bail are remanded into either local authority accommodation or into the prison system. The option used depends on the defendant's age and the availability of local authority accommodation. Children younger than 15 years cannot be remanded to prison. The Criminal Justice Act 1991 (s62) made provision for the eventual abolition of remands to prison for 15 and 16 year-old boys. However, 15 and 16 year-old girls cannot be remanded into prison custody.

Courts must abide by s44(1) of the Children and Young Persons Act 1933 when a child or young person is brought before them. They must *have regard to the welfare of the child . . .and shall take proper steps for removing [them] from undesirable surroundings and for securing that proper provision is made for [their] education...*

Most children under 18 years are brought before specially constituted magistrates' courts known as youth courts. Youth courts try a wider range of offences than ordinary magistrates' courts. Children must always be tried in a youth court unless they are: charged with homicide, over 14 years and charged with an offence for which an adult would receive 14 years imprisonment or more; or they are charged jointly with someone over 18 years and then they should stand trial in a crown court.

Sentences available for 10-13 year-olds

- Absolute discharge
- Conditional discharge
- Bind over
  (of offender or parent)
- Fine (for which parent can be made responsible)
- Compensation order
  (for which parent can be made responsible)
- Attendance centre order

- Supervision order
- Supervision order with requirements including psychiatric treatment, educational requirements, night restrictions, specified activities or residence requirements
- Detention under s53 of Children and Young Persons Act for manslaughter or murder.

Only 6% of all known offenders aged 10-13 were dealt with by the courts. Of those sentenced for an indictable offence, 1,300 or 54% were given an absolute or conditional discharge.

There is currently no uniform age for the beginning of criminal responsibility across Europe. In England and Wales, criminal responsibility begins at the age of 10. In the Netherlands, children aged 12 are considered to be responsible, while in France that age is 13; in Austria, Germany and Italy 14; in Sweden 15 and in Spain and Belgium 18 years.

© The Howard League for Penal Reform 1994

10-13 year-olds sentenced for indictable offences, 1992		
	Boys	Girls
Absolute or conditional discharge	1,200	100
Fine	200	0
Supervision order	400	0
Attendance centre order	500	0
Total	**2,300**	**100**

Source: Criminal Statistics England and Wales 1992

35 per cent of all males have been convicted of a criminal offence by the age of 35

Young people aged 16-24 are the most frequent victims of assaults and personal thefts

The average age of a burglar is 17

One young man in eleven has a conviction for theft by the time he reaches his 17th birthday

46 per cent of all recorded crime is committed by males under 21

The peak age of offending for boys and girls is 15; 20 per cent of young offenders are aged under 17

One quarter of car crime is committed by boys aged 10-16

(Source: Crime Concern)

From vandals in Newcastle to louts in Guildford

'Yob culture' is here, but need it be here to stay? Latest research suggests not

*By Peter Hetherington
and Angella Johnson*

Newcastle: police are trying to build bridges with street gangs on the Scotswood estate, and say the word 'yob' is not appropriate for young people with no hope of a job.

Behind the derelict, burned-out houses, PC Martin Abbott confronts a youth and his accomplice suspected of arson, joy-riding and street crime. 'You set fire to those houses?' he asks. The boyish 17 year-old protests his innocence with a curt 'nah'.

'Well, you've taken cars away – how many? 20-30?'

'But I've had a mini,' he replies. 'Legit. I've applied for a provisional licence.'

'But you're banned for how long – 20 years?' the constable reminds him as a young housing officer alongside counts the cost of a violent street culture over the past year.

In this corner of the Scotswood estate in Newcastle upon Tyne, 20 houses have been gutted in 12 months, with tenants often driven away by vandalism or intimidation from gangs.

But yobs? PC Abbott and his colleague Richard Berry say the label is inappropriate for the youths terrorising an estate which embraces a high proportion of single parents and suffers from endemic unemployment, as a result of which family structures and social order have broken down.

'They've got huge problems, their family backgrounds are appalling – but yobs? I don't think so,' says PC Abbott.

'It's a nice blanket phrase that covers a multitude of sins,' volunteers Sergeant Steve Young, back at the small police station.

'A yob, I reckon, is a grown man who knows the difference between right and wrong and goes ahead and does it,' chips in another constable.

In parts of Newcastle and other inner-city areas around the country, PC Abbott thinks that a street culture verging on the violent and the criminal has become perfectly normal for disaffected youth. 'To them it is quite natural to trash empty houses,' he says.

As the Government attacks 'yobbism' in the run-up to the Tory conference, some officers find it hard to disguise their contempt for politicians playing the crime card yet again.

'This street culture has a life of its own,' says PC Berry. 'It's not so much a legal problem as a social issue and it's too simplistic to brand it a yob culture.'

'Even though some of them have got long criminal records, when you talk to them they're not always bad people.

The sergeant adds: 'Locking up kids is easy. We could arrest them all the time for breaches of the peace, but they'll be back again on the street the night after.'

The Scotswood community police team has been attempting to break down the gang culture with a series of non-confrontational initiatives beginning with an operation codenamed 'sheepdog'.

While hardened criminals have been targeted through painstaking surveillance, attempts have been made to build bridges with the jobless street gangs in Newcastle's West End.

Working in partnership with the city council and youth and voluntary agencies under the umbrella of a City Challenge initiative, police believe they are turning the tide.

With officers back on the beat, overall crime fell by 13 per cent this year between January and August, with house burglaries down by 20 per cent. Joy-riding offences have dropped by 16 per cent, with similar falls in assaults and vehicle thefts.

But Superintendent David Swift, the local police commander, says that, unless more funding is found, officers might have to leave the streets when City Challenge ends in 1997.

Guildford

'Town centre faces a continual menace' say locals – 'they swarm like flies when the shops shut' – but the authorities have a different perspective.

When a 'fly-on-the-wall' TV camera crew went on night patrol with police in Guildford, Surrey, they captured footage of drunken teenagers – some only 14 – rampaging through the town centre.

The police described it as a one-off but the locals claim it was the latest in a long period of continuing young, loutish behaviour in the town centre.

'They swarm into town like flies once the shops shut,' says Murray Franklin, 42, who lives in a nearby village but occasionally meets friends for a drink in the town.

'It is mostly boys but there are some girls. They are rowdy, rude, and generally disrespectful to adults going about their business.' His L registration car has been broken into twice in the past year in a car park.

The local police and borough council argue that youth crime is no worse than any comparable large town. But some senior residents are plainly scared to wander around after dark.

'It can get pretty intimidating,' says shop manager Joy Riddle, 50.

She has lived here all her life and remembers when vandalism was rare. 'We were a small community. Everyone knew each other and you could tell a youngster off, knowing the parents would back you. Today we have a university and a couple of colleges. You hardly recognise a face in the crowd. I have heard about the drunkenness and fighting.' On her way to work in the mornings she occasionally sees the evidence – blood-spattered pavements.

'We were broken into six times between September and December last year,' she said. 'Now, like even the smallest businesses around here, we are as fortified as any bank.'

Patricia Mayhew, in her 50s, blames declining moral standards and a lack of respect. 'Nowadays young people seem to think the world owes them something. The economic climate and bleak future prospects do not help any.'

Guildford, with its assortment

of pubs and three night clubs which can cater for 3,000 is a mecca for Surrey's young. To help calm fears, the council is to install closed circuit television in the city centre, among other measures.

There were 3,000 reported cases of petty crimes last year – Guildford's population is 127,000 and the borough's chief executive, David Watts, said: 'Of course there have been isolated incidents of juvenile crime but mostly the problem is one of perception. We are doing our best to put that right in consultation with night club owners, the police, and pub landlords.'

Mrs Riddle said that the closure of the Horse and Groom public house, a haunt of boisterous squaddies from nearby Aldershot, 'certainly helped to cut down on some of the drunken brawls.' The pub was one of two bombed in 1974.

A boy's view of right and wrong

BBC Radio 4's *File on Four* interviewed Boy C earlier this year
to see if he knew it was wrong to damage a moped

Questioner: 'Do you have an idea in your mind of what is right and wrong?'

C: 'Yeah.'
Q: 'What is right and wrong?'
C: 'Robbing cars is wrong.'
Q: 'Why is it wrong?'
C: 'It's taking somebody else's things.'
Q: When you were 12, there was this incident, did you know what was right and wrong?'
C: 'Yeah, and I never done nothing wrong. I was right. I was only looking. They (the police) said I had a crowbar. I never had a crowbar. They was telling lies through their teeth.'
Q: 'If you had been stealing or had been trying to take that motorbike would you have known that was wrong?'

File on Four
BBC Radio Four

C: 'Yeah, of course.'
Q: 'How would you have known that?'
C: 'I'm not stupid.'
Q: 'When do you think you learned what was right and wrong?'
C: 'In the infants, when I was younger.'
Q: 'Do you think most young people of 12 would know right and wrong?'
C: 'I don't know. Some are thick. Some don't know the difference.'
Q: 'Who taught you what's right and wrong?'

C: 'My mum and dad, school, my nan, grandad.'

Police told the BBC that Boy C had been offending since he was nine. By 12, as part of a gang taking vehicles and stealing from shops, he had committed at least 20 offences of theft. Since 1992 he had continued to offend.

Boy C was again asked why he had offended when he knew it was wrong.
C: 'Dunno. Because everybody else was doing it. It's when you're there with all your mates and that, they're doing it, you do it.'
Q: 'Do you regret it now?'
C: 'Yeah, going to court and all that.'

Experts call for a system to deal with young offenders

Stephen Ward examines some concerns the judgment raises

Many experts in child development and criminology expressed concern yesterday that the law restored by the Law Lords left it to the courts to make complex psychological judgments about the moral awareness of a young child.

Many believed too that the existing penal system is not seen as the best way to deliver the appropriate punishment or treatment to stop child offenders inevitably becoming adult villains.

Paul Cavadino, chairman of the Penal Affairs Consortium – an umbrella group of 24 organisations, last night welcomed the age of criminality being raised again from 10. He said: 'In most other West European countries, and throughout the USA, children of this age who commit offences do not appear before criminal courts. They are dealt with by civil court proceedings concerned with the need for compulsory measures of care.

'In particularly serious cases this can include long-term detention in secure accommodation. Many foreign commentators are amazed that children of this age, accused of serious offences, can be dealt with by an adult-style crown court criminal trial.'

According to the National Children's Bureau, criminal responsibility starts at 14 in Germany, 15 in Denmark and Sweden, 16 in Spain and 18 in Belgium. The bureau says society could be protected from child killers, such as the murderers of the Liverpool toddler James Bulger, under the care provisions in section 31 of the 1989 Children Act. In Scotland the age is eight.

Allan Levy QC, a barrister specialising in child law, described the compromise as 'a sneaking recognition that 10 as an age is too low, but without the fortitude to alter the law.

'In this range between 10 and 14 there's a presumption of no responsibility, but the prosecution are given the opportunity to prove it.'

Mr Levy believes there is a danger that magistrates and judges might look at the social background of the child and decide that a middle-class offender was more likely to know right from wrong.

Robert Broudie, the solicitor representing Boy C – the child in the Law Lords' judgment – thought that the majority of children over 10 did know the difference between right and wrong, but the Lords compromise was about right.

He said: 'You must have safeguards. It would have been terrible in the Bulger case if the prosecution had not had to prove that the two boys who killed him knew that what they were doing was wrong.

'It's important in a civilised society to recognise the differences between a child and an adult.'

But he added that it was a 'difficult area' to try to draw that line. He was adamant that, if criminality were to be lowered, there had to be a wider change. 'I think it is preferable for there to be a separate system to deal with children.'

Medical experts agree that the age of criminality is a difficult one to define. Dr Susan Bailey, a forensic psychiatrist who has dealt with hundreds of child criminals including 20 who have killed, believes that most 10 year-old offenders have not reached full moral maturity and that there is a wide range between different children of the same age.

'Between the age of 10 and 14, there is a tremendous range of developments within youngsters,' she told BBC Radio 4's *File on Four* programme.

'They develop cognitively, emotionally and psychologically, and I think one of the key elements is that during that time most youngsters develop the capacity to move from concrete thinking to abstract thinking. The ability to have abstract thoughts is associated with your ability to think through what the consequences of the action are when you're committing a crime. So it is a critical and central area.'

© *The Independent*
March, 1995

Youth culture linked to rise in delinquency

By Martin Whitfield

The development of a separate youth culture could be responsible for the rapid post-war rise in anti-social behaviour, according to a new study.

Professor Sir Michael Rutter, head of the Department of Child and Adolescent Psychiatry at the London Institute of Psychiatry, said the development of psychological disorders had occurred at a time of economic boom and could not be attributed to worsening living conditions.

'Young people have become a separate class,' he said. 'They have their own culture, their own dress and music and have less contact with other age groups.'

The report suggests that marking adolescents off as a separate group runs the risk of reducing the influence of adults on their behaviour and increasing the power of the peer group.

However, Sir Michael warned against seeking a single solution to a problem that had occurred across the industrialised world. 'It would seem that something as striking as this ought to have a simple explanation and it's very frustrating that that's not what comes out of the study,' he said.

Written by Sir Michael and David Smith, Professor of Criminology at the University of Edinburgh, the study examined suicides, drug and alcohol use, anorexia nervosa and bulimia and crime among 12 to 26 year-olds. It found:

- Substantial increases in disorders in nearly all countries during the past 50 years.
- The rise was sudden. There were no similar increases earlier in the century despite urbanisation and unemployment.

Photo: Ulrike Preuss/Format

- As psychosocial disorders were increasing, physical health was improving.
- Suicide rates showed the highest increase among young males, with rates up to three times that of females.
- Steadily rising levels of drug dependency.
- All the major psychosocial disorders studied began or peaked during teenage years. Criminal behaviour was most common among 17 year-olds.

Several tentative causes are put forward including family break-ups, longer adolescence, a more consumerist society and greater individualism.

Mr Smith said there was a paradox that the rise in social disorders had occurred during the 'golden era' of economic expansion. Although unemployment and poverty were useful in explaining individual behaviour, they provided no guide to the causes over time. Crime had risen in most societies, although Japan – which had experienced the most dramatic growth rates between 1950 and 1973 – experienced a fall in reported crime over a 40-year period to 1990.

Unemployment statistics over time did not correlate with disorder and a general increase in unemployment in the 1970s and 1980s had not been associated with a similar rise in the rate of increase of disorder.

Family discord and divorce were said to have been influential but it appeared the main risk was from parental confrontation, rather than the act of divorce.

The changing nature of adolescence was highlighted as one of the most important factors as children enter puberty earlier but are not accepted as adults until much later. 'Lengthened adolescence might mean the prolongation of an insecure status, and of an uncertain personal identity. It might lead to internal conflicts and to clashes with paternal or other authority,' the study says.

Sir Michael said the research presented an exciting challenge. 'If there has been such a marked rise over time, then it ought be possible to provide an equally dramatic fall if we understood the processes that underlined the rise.'

Psychosocial disorders in young people; Sir Michael Rutter and David Smith; published by John Wiley and Sons on behalf of Academia Europaea; £49.95.

From the cradle to criminality

What makes a violent criminal? Dr Simon Wessely on research that throws new light on this question

There are few more controversial areas of research than the causes of violent crime, which so often come down to polemics on the lines of nature versus nurture.

Simple genetic explanations, such as the claim that violent males had an extra Y chromosome, are now discredited. Nevertheless, more careful work has continued to support the idea of a genetic contribution. Much of this research has taken place in Scandinavia, not because the Swedes or Danes are more violent, but because those countries possess superb data systems, including twin registers, essential for the conduct of proper genetic research.

Studies comparing identical and non-identical twins, and also the outcome of adopted children, have provided convincing evidence of a modest genetic contribution to crime. Another line of inquiry has looked at the effect of early brain damage, such as might be acquired at birth, and found a link with later violent crime.

Nowadays nobody would claim that either genetics or brain damage is the cause of violent crime or that social factors such as the family environment are unimportant. There is no doubt that the ways parents deal with their children plays a crucial role in the development of criminal behaviour. Modern researchers no longer ask the question of nurture, but instead how nurture influences nature – what factors are involved in the pathways from birth to later criminality.

A report in the latest issue of *Archives of General Psychiatry* provides one answer. Adrian Raine and colleagues at the University of Southern California have studied all the 4,629 males born at the maternity hospital in Copenhagen between 1959 and 1961. The Danish hospitals keep meticulous records of the circumstances of delivery and any possible complications. One year later, all the children were followed up and further information obtained on the home and family circumstances.

The research team then linked this information with the Danish National Criminal Register, which records all police contacts and criminal convictions for all Danish citizens. By the age of 19, 16 per cent of the males had a criminal record, with 3 per cent having a conviction for a violent offence.

There is no doubt that the ways parents deal with their children plays a crucial role in the development of criminal behaviour

Dr Raine, who comes from the North East of England, thus created a unique opportunity to study the links between birth complications, family environment and later violent criminality. He first found that those who had experienced birth complications alone did not have an increased risk of violent offending.

Those whose birth had been normal, but who had suffered parental rejection, which the researchers defined as either an unwanted pregnancy, failed attempts to abort the pregnancy, or the infant being sent to a public institution in the first year of life, were also no more at risk.

However, those who had both a difficult delivery and then had experienced parental rejection were substantially more likely to end up with a conviction for violent offences. Furthermore, difficult deliveries combined with parental rejection were associated later only with violent crime and not with crime in general.

This research is a milestone in understanding the links between early environment and later behaviour. The authors postulate that birth complications result in early, albeit slight, brain damage that is associated with difficulties in learning and with self-control. These might lead to later difficulties at school, and then with employment.

Problems start to develop if this predisposition is linked with a disruption to the normal process of bonding between mother and child. Poor early bonding may be associated with later difficulties in emotional relationships, and a reduced capacity to express and feel affection. It is the combination of the early damage to the central nervous system succeeded by further disruption in the normal development of personality and feeling that is important.

Writing in this week's *British Medical Journal*, David Farrington of the Institute of Criminology at Cambridge, and Professor Jonathan Shepherd, a Cardiff surgeon with an interest in the effects of violence, conclude that, although much of the research on crime prevention has concentrated on the availability of weapons and better protection of premises and vehicles, early interventions, such as increasing family support and pre-school education, are also effective in reducing later offending.

The new research from Denmark adds to the case that increasing the care-giving skills of parents at risk might also intervene to break the links between biological predisposition and later violent offending.

Dr Simon Wessely is senior lecturer in psychological medicine at King's College School of Medicine.

© The Times
February, 1995

Scientist denounces criminal gene theory

By Tom Wilkie
Science Editor

A private meeting of scientists who believe that the roots of criminality are anchored in human genes has been condemned as 'troublesome, disturbing and unbalanced'.

Much of the research 'would be scientifically unacceptable in the context of animal behaviour, yet it is given a veneer of respectability in the human context,' according to Steven Rose, professor of biology at the Open University based in Milton Keynes, Buckinghamshire.

The controversial meeting in London this week is organised by the international Ciba Foundation. It will be dominated by American psychologists, and outsiders are barred. Critics of the 'criminal genes' position do not appear on the participants' list.

Professor Rose, who is a long-standing critic of the belief that individual differences in human behaviour have a genetic not an environmental basis and wrote in this month's *Nature* journal that genetic determinism offers no solutions to what are essentially society's problems, pointed out that when the United States National Institutes of Health tried to organise a similar event 'the political furore was so great, it had to be cancelled. It was seen as overtly racist'.

The chairman of the meeting, Professor Sir Michael Rutter, of the Institute of Psychiatry in London, was unavailable for comment. Press inquiries were referred to the Ciba Foundation which said that all the participants had been told not to comment in advance of the meeting.

Professor Rose questioned the definition of 'criminal and anti-social behaviour' being analysed at the meeting. 'They are nearly always thinking about working-class crime, and do not mention white-collar crimes such as fraud or wife-beating among middle-class men. The definition has a social and class bias,' he said.

He admits 'it is improbable that genes are not involved,' but he does not believe they are the real determining causes of crime. Even accepting the meeting's definition of crime, he said, 'Violence in British society has risen dramatically over the past decade. In the US, the homicide rate among young males has doubled since 1985. There is no conceivable genetic explanation for that – this isn't a sudden mutant gene appearing.'

Researchers have tried to infer that behaviour is genetically based

Apart from a Dutch study which has traced a behavioural problem through three generations of one family to a specific biochemical defect, most of the research being discussed during the meeting does not actually focus on human DNA.

Instead, researchers have tried to infer that behaviour is genetically based by studying statistical similarities and differences between identical and non-identical twins. Historically, however, twin studies of traits such as intelligence have failed to withstand scientific scrutiny.

The eminent Oxford moral philosopher, Jonathan Glover, will be talking to the conference about the implications of precise genetic explanations of human behaviour for our concepts of blame and responsibility. 'There is a timebomb under our moral thinking – determinism,' he said. He does not see a great difference between genetic or environ-mental causes of behaviour: 'If we seek to explain the characteristics that make people praiseworthy or blameworthy, then ultimately we are driven back to factors that are not under their control.'

Mr Glover feels that we may have to resort to an aesthetic appreciation of people's character, rather as we judge their physical looks as beautiful or ugly: 'We ought to give up the metaphysical assumption that character is something for which people are responsible,' he said.

© *The Independent*

SOMEONE TOLD HIM THAT HIS CRIMINALITY IS IN HIS JEANS

Companies beware: computer crime can dent your profits

They don't carry guns or knives, and they don't use getaway cars, but this growing band of criminals is able to make off with goods worth thousands of pounds, and they can often do it in seconds

by Brian Hanney

They are the silent but deadly practitioners of computer crime, an area of villainy that has been expanding for a decade, but which the law enforcers around the world are now tackling head on.

In Britain, hundreds of companies are at risk from computer criminals. While exact figures are difficult to obtain, they are probably costing public bodies and industry millions of pounds annually.

But in the UK, at least, theft of computer data is not always an arm of organised crime.

Police regularly come across cases of quite junior employees who take advantage of their own company's lax security to embezzle valuable information, which they can use for themselves or sell on to unscrupulous rivals.

One of the problems police forces have in stamping out this crime is the attitude of those they are trying to protect. 'Many employers just don't realise how easy it is to access vital information and don't take the necessary precautions,' said one police officer.

Industrial espionage has been around as long as there has been industry.

Similarly with computer crime, the growth of 'hacking' – unauthorised access to computer data – came as some systems experts, amateur and professional, thought that they could use their skills more profitably on the other side of the law.

Like many branches of crime, data theft began in a big way in the United States back in the seventies.

Here in Britain, the dangers of computer crime were recognised in the early eighties and in 1984 the Metropolitan Police set up their own Computer Crime Unit to devote energies full-time to tackling the threat.

An important step was taken in 1990 to codify the crime with the Computer Misuse Act. This created three new offences dealing with different aspects of computer misuse.

Section 1 deals with the widespread problem of hacking, and conviction carries a fine of £2,000 and/or up to six months in jail.

The more serious Section 2 covers unauthorised access of a computer with the aim of committing 'or to facilitate the commission of' a serious crime such as fraud or theft. It carries a maximum jail term of five years and/or an unlimited fine.

Section 3 outlaws 'unauthorised modification' of computer information. This crime is best known to office-workers in the form of 'viruses' – hidden instructions designed to distort or destroy a legitimate computer program.

This crime often takes the form of pure 'mischief-making', with viruses such as 'logic bombs' that will make pages of script disintegrate, and are often timed to go off around traditional anniversaries such as Valentine's Day.

But the authorities do not view the crime as a joke and, like Section 2, it is punishable by up to five years' imprisonment and/or an unlimited fine. Both Section 2 and 3 offences are triable at the Crown Court.

Detective Constable Mark Morris is one of the four-strong team at the Computer Crime Unit based in the City of London. His unit deals with all aspects of computer crime except the physical theft of computers – but more than a quarter of cases involve viruses.

Under threat

He believes the dozen or so convictions made each year are 'just the tip of the iceberg'.

He says: 'If we employed 100 people they would all be busy in a couple of months.'

Under threat are not just high-tech multi-million pound businesses, but hospitals, councils and even small workshops and retail outlets.

But more police training time is being spent studying computer crime and most police forces have specialists able to undertake investigations. Successful prosecutions can take months and even years of patient work. But, when they reach court, they usually result in conviction.

A recent case in Croydon, south London, involved a gang who were cloning illegally obtained mobile numbers onto stolen mobile phones, using computer technology.

Three people were convicted and received jail sentences of 12 months, eight months and six months.

DC Morris says the severity of the sentences reflects the growing awareness by courts of the danger posed by this crime.

But, as with all crime, prevention is more important than legal remedy, and businesses are taking the problem more seriously, helped by advice from the police and the Home Office.

Part of the problem is the growth of computer 'literacy', which brings the inevitable downside of technically minded villains.

Chilling tales of 14 year-old adolescents hacking into the Pentagon's top-secret defence systems are thankfully fanciful. But, however complex a system, there is usually someone determined enough to try to challenge it.

Determined hackers

DC Morris says: 'There's a whole generation of youngsters who have been brought up on computers since they were toddlers. They would think it unusual not to have one in the home.

'I'd say in a few years time it will be normal to use Internet technology to help with homework or research.'

Of course, very few of these youngsters will turn to crime, but it

The American experience

Computer technology has grown faster and more furiously in the United States than else where, leading to the worldwide dominance of the giant IBM, known as 'The Big Blue'. Hot on its heels has come the criminal.

Until 1984, computer crimes were prosecuted under various sections of the federal or criminal code. But that year Congress passed the Counterfeit Access Device and Computer Fraud and Abuse Act, followed two years later by an amendment to 'clarify and strengthen' the earlier measure.

Among the prohibitions of the 1986 Act are obtaining information relating to 'national defence or foreign relations' and financial records.

Despite laws protecting so-called 'federal interest' computers – those belonging to the government or financial institutions – prosecutions have been few.

Experts believe that, similar to the British experience, owners prefer to handle security problems themselves to avoid the embarrassment of a trial which could expose the system's vulnerability.

But, here lagging behind the UK, it was not until 1991 that the Department of Justice set up the Computer Crime Unit. Its main function has been to lobby and advise on computer crime rather than carry out prosecutions.

Many states outlaw what they call 'computer voyeurism'. This means it is an offence simply to examine the contents of a computer system, even if there is no attempt to make changes or extract data. The laws are designed to protect individual privacy.

Piracy of computer software alone is reckoned to cost US producers $12 billion annually.

takes just a handful of determined hackers to cause mayhem.

And hacking has become 'like a huge club for some people,' says DC Morris. So, for a company, the costs can be high, but exact figures remain difficult to come by. This could cost firms thousands of pounds – and the expense of bringing in experts to track down the crime can also be high since this usually requires meticulous and painstaking work. As DC Morris says: 'The bigger the company the bigger the crime gets.'

Unfortunately, computer crime is set to increase, simply because more and more screens are appearing in offices.

Twenty years ago electronic gadgetry was a rare sight in all but the most sophisticated of offices. Now more screens mean more theft.

Invisible crime

But the growth in this 'armchair' crime has one peculiar side-effect. Cases of the traditional crime of

armed robbery are going down – and the growth in computer crime is the probable cause.

A major form of computer crime, for instance, is credit card fraud, which costs the banking industry millions each year.

Replacing the man in the stockinged mask and cash is the lone hacker, who could be stealing thousands working from the bedroom of a rural cottage.

While this is obviously positive news for the safety of security guards, bank personnel and others, the very 'invisibility' of the crime leads banks themselves to be secretive about it.

'Often when a computer data base has been hacked into, the victim company might be reluctant to admit it,' says DC Morris. With traditional crimes, the loss – in both human and financial terms – is all too apparent.

Banks and other large financial institutions naturally fear the vulnerability of their computer systems being exposed.

This in turn leads to their reluctance to accept the reality of 'phantom withdrawals' from cash machines, for example. Instances where money has been taken out from individuals' bank accounts are of growing concern to consumer groups.

It is the job of banks and building societies constantly to improve their security, and the job of the police and other specialists to help them do that.

Scotland Yard's Computer Crime Unit has the task not only of solving the crime, but of ensuring that firms and other bodies admit that a crime has taken place.

'The message is to educate the community that, when they report unauthorised access, it will be treated in the strictest confidence,' says DC Moms.

'People in the business community can't complain if they don't report it to the police.' This trust is crucial to gain the co-operation of companies which handle hundreds of thousands of pounds daily.

Potential damage

He believes people must accept that technology is here to stay and understand its increasing importance in almost every aspect of life.

He says: 'All people in industry must realise the power of technology and the damage it can do when misused.'

With so much controlled by computers it is 'frightening' to think what people can do, he adds. The potential for crime has increased with computerisation.

But this also highlights the other important area of data protection, where the Home Office has recently moved to tighten up the law.

The Data Protection Act of 1984 was a response to the dangers posed by the ever-growing amount of information stored on computer databases.

The Act makes it an offence 'knowingly or recklessly' to disclose information to an unauthorised person.

But former Home Office Minister Lord Ferrers recently brought in an amendment to the Criminal Justice Bill to close a legal loophole.

Safeguard your software

So what can you do to ensure you do not fall prey to computer crime? The Metropolitan Police's Computer Crime Unit has prepared a leaflet in conjunction with IBM and PC Plus containing a number of sensible tips on protecting your computer from the criminal.

To protect your data:
- Remember to back up your data on a regular basis
- Don't forget about 'write-protect' tabs on disks
- Always label and back up your disks
- Exposure to heat, magnetism, dust and sunlight can cause damage to disks and loss of data

To prevent unauthorised access:
- Unauthorised access is a criminal offence, punishable by imprisonment or a large fine
- Use password protection wherever possible
- Use a warning notice to remind unauthorised users that they are breaking the law
- Be aware of the Data Protection Act

To prevent virus infection:
- Regularly use anti-virus scanning software. Beware of untried and untested diskettes
- Be cautious of suspect or unknown sources of software

To protect your PC:
- Use your computer locking devices and secure your premises
- Security mark equipment and record serial numbers. Take extra care with laptop and notebook PCs
- Treat your computer like the valuable asset it is

For information on IBM security offerings, tel: 0345 989393. To find out more about computer and virus offences, telephone the Met's Computer Crime Unit on 0171-230 1177

This makes it an offence to *obtain* information such as bank or credit card details or medical records by trickery or deception.

Lord Ferrers explained that the amendment would 'make the tricksters think twice'.

But he also stressed that the main responsibility still lies with commercial organisations 'to take proper steps to protect their own information'.

Thankfully, industry is starting to play its part in all areas of the protection of computer information.

While the Institute of Directors says it has not examined the issue in detail, the broader-based Confederation of British Industry produced a report in 1991 in conjunction with accountants Ernst & Young with information on how businesses could safeguard their systems.

Unfortunately, no updated policy statements have been produced since.

A spokeswoman admits this is probably to do with the recession, which has concentrated business minds elsewhere.

'It's not been given the same priority. Other things have taken over,' she says.

But interest in the issue is likely to return, particularly as the police 'hammer home' the message that they 'must have close contact with most of the big companies'.

As D C Moms says: 'We sometimes need expert technical help, and who better than the guys from the companies?'

As that message gets home, and the police and business see closer co-operation, life could get increasingly uncomfortable for the villain of high-tech.

Met's Computer Crime Unit on 0171-230 1177.

© *Crime Prevention News* *December, 1994*

Crime gangs use Internet to access credit card fraud

Computer transactions allow numbers to be hijacked and used to buy goods

By Charles Arthur
Technology Correspondent

Organised gangs are using the Internet to steal credit card numbers and exploit flaws in bank credit checking systems to buy goods and services internationally. In Britain alone this fraud is worth thousands of pounds a week.

The criminals first use a 'sniffer' program, which they run on computers that route data over the Internet, to capture credit card numbers when people order goods over the network.

Because the US government has restricted the use and export of encryption programs, the card details are not encrypted. The criminals set a program to search for strings of numbers 16 digits long separated by spaces – the standard form for a credit card number. These are then transferred to other computers for fraudulent use.

Card owners are not aware their details have been captured until false purchases show up on their bill.

The criminals also make credit checks harder by moving the card details between countries.

Another option they use is a program that randomly generates patterns of numbers matching those of a credit card.

'We have had scares in the past few months with batches of numbers being collected and passed over the Internet,' said Roger Alexander, head of the division within Barclays Bank which investigates new market technologies. 'But we would make it clear that for someone to send their credit card number unencrypted over the Internet breaks their agreement with the bank that issued the card.'

In Britain, US card numbers are frequently used to order high-value items from computer mail-order companies. The criminals rely on two weaknesses in banks' checking systems: the card has not been reported stolen and American banks refuse to let mail-order companies check the address of the card's owner. The bank therefore authorises the transaction and the mail-order company has to honour the purchase.

Typically the criminals order add-on computer memory because it is small yet valuable. One company in Purley, Surrey, became suspicious when a caller gave the name 'Michael Bolton', a card number from a US bank and ordered more than £1,000 worth of memory chips for delivery to a north London address. The issuing bank authorised the payment but the company contacted the police. They tried to catch the caller at the delivery address but failed. The goods were never delivered.

Mail-order computer companies contacted by *the Independent* say that they have lobbied the banks which issue credit cards 'for years' to improve their checking systems.

Robert Littas, in charge of risk management at Visa International, said: 'We are aware of this and that it's an area of contention. But we don't know how big a problem it is.'

Worldwide, credit card fraud costs banks and retailers an estimated $1.5bn (£1bn).

Both Visa and high street banks say that people should not use the Internet to order items because the lack of encryption makes fraud feasible.

Barclays Merchant Services this week launched Barclay Square (sic), a shopping mall on the Internet's World Wide Web which uses encryption technology to scramble credit card numbers before they are sent. 'This encryption method has been rigorously tested and we look forward to it catching on,' Mr Alexander said.

But Rob Smith, who has a Web site called UK Shopping Centre, said: 'Their system only works with one piece of software. Until somebody comes up with a standard encryption system that everyone can use, there's little point in any organisation jumping in with their own format.'

The criminals use a 'sniffer' program to capture credit card numbers

© The Independent
June, 1995

Children taught crime on Internet

Computer schoolboys drawn into credit fraud.
By Neil Darbyshire and Christine McGourty

Police said yesterday that the Internet global computer network was teaching children how to commit serious crimes after six boys from an independent school admitted using the system to organise a sophisticated credit card fraud against mail-order firms.

The incident, involving pupils at Highgate School, north London, highlights the complete lack of control over what can be placed on the system, which links computers around the world.

Bomb-making recipes and formulae for making napalm and the drug Ecstasy can all be found on the Internet, along with price lists for illegal drugs and limitless supplies of free, hard-core pornography.

'This Internet is absolute dynamite and it is without any form of quality control,' said Det Insp Ron Laverick. of the Metropolitan Police, who investigated the credit card fraud.

'Young people are being taught how to commit crimes, and you only have to imagine the potential for paedophiles, terrorists and pornography.'

The boys, aged 15 and 16, learned how to perpetrate the credit fraud from a 12-page bulletin entitled 'The Basics of Carding', put on the Internet by an unknown American calling himself 'The Metallian'.

They keyed into the appropriate number while using their own home computers to 'surf the Net', the expression used by enthusiasts for keying into the system.

They then bought watches, training shoes, computer games and electronic equipment worth several thousand pounds from mail-order and catalogue companies, using credit card numbers from discarded receipts obtained from a local restaurant.

'These are very nice, bright kids from very nice families who have had temptation put in their way and have fallen victim to this ridiculous system,' Det Insp Laverick said.

'They could all now have criminal convictions and their parents have gone through hell.'

He said the boys were likely to be cautioned rather than charged, but added that future offenders may not be so lucky.

The fraud was discovered when the parents of one of the boys became suspicious after boxes of mail-order goods began arriving at his home in Hampstead Garden Suburb and reported the matter to the police.

'Some were having things sent to the homes of relatives and friends, but because they didn't have any criminal sophistication, a lot of the things were sent to their own homes,' Det Insp Laverick said.

Richard Longhurst, editor of *Net*, a specialist Internet magazine, said the subject of controlling information held on the network had been discussed at a recent meeting of the G7 countries, but he added that such control would be difficult to achieve.

Did you know?

CARD FRAUD LOSSES

Average loss per plastic card before reported lost/stolen **£250**

Average loss per plastic card after reported lost/stolen **£330**

Average total loss per plastic card used fraudulently **£580**

The above is an extract from ALERT
© APACS

FRAUD FACTS

Number of cards lost or stolen each day **5000**

Number of cards lost or stolen each hour **280**

Fraud loss per second **£4**

The above is an extract from ALERT
© APACS

'I don't really know how they would stop people putting this sort of information on,' he said. 'I can set up my computer here, log on to a computer in another country, which could issue instructions to a computer in a third country to download information to a computer in a fourth country.

'If there was an offence involved in the process, where would it have been committed and who would have jurisdiction?'

Richard Kennedy, head master of Highgate School, said the boys involved were all bright pupils and that this was a case of 'experimentation which went too far'.

Because the offences were not committed at the school or by using school equipment, he said he would take no action against the boys and that it was essentially a matter for the police.

'I think everyone is aware that there have been problems as the Internet has developed, with its

massive potential for storing information,' he said.

'It is no surprise that there are unscrupulous people who put this sort of information on to bulletin boards, which are completely uncontrolled, and that clever, and some times naive, young people experiment with the system. 'We must depend on new kinds of vigilance and care to be taken by parents and schools over how much access to give young people to the Internet.'

Different techniques for making atomic bombs are among the extraordinary data that can be obtained.

The electronic version of a journal called *Anarchy 'n' Explosives*, also on the system, contains instructions on making TNT, nitroglycerine and dynamite.

At the electronic address *alt. suicide*, there is a comprehensive guide to suicide.

The numbers of stolen phone charge cards have also been traded for money on the Internet, along with illegally-copied software, particularly computer games.

Pornography is everywhere, most of it scanned in from magazines.

Prof Stephen Heppell, of Anglia Polytechnic University, involved in an Internet schools project, said: 'The children have access to everything. But we do put computers in a sociable setting, so they are used in groups. At home, the computer should be in the kitchen or living room rather than in a bedroom.'

Chilli order led to a £1,000 sting

Charles Arthur finds a World-Wide Web user who is more wary now

Rory Sutherland thought he had used the Internet simply to order a $10 (£6.35) bottle of chilli sauce from a California company. So he was surprised when MasterCard called him a few weeks later to ask if he was buying almost £1,000 worth of computer equipment from a mail-order company in Newbury, Berkshire.

Mr Sutherland had been using the Internet for only six months when he joined the growing ranks who have had their credit card details stolen by a 'sniffer' program set up by a criminal. He feels sure that is what happened, because as an advertising executive at Ogilvy & Mather Direct, he almost always uses his American Express card – they are a client.

But he used his MasterCard to order the chilli from a site on the World-Wide Web, part of the Internet that displays text and pictures together, and is increasingly used to offer goods and services. 'I remember that site was one of the few places on the Web which didn't accept Amex,' he recalls. He filled in a form on the screen of his computer in London, including his name, credit card number and its expiry date, and pressed a key to transmit it over the global computer network.

'It's easier than ordering by phone, especially if the company is in the US,' he explains. 'The prices are often better, and you don't have to make an international call.'

But the details he sent were not encrypted, so anyone who intercepted them could use his credit card with impunity. It is comparatively easy for a criminal with programming skills to get a computer that routes data on the Internet to watch for numbers that are 16 digits long – the typical form for a credit card – and record them for later use.

'I think I made a mistake in giving my credit card number in clusters of four figures separated by spaces,' Mr Sutherland says ruefully.

It was lucky for him that he lives in Britain: if he lived in the US, the order would almost certainly have gone through, because the card would not have been reported as missing.

'I'm more wary now,' Mr Sutherland says. 'But it was just one freakish experience, a one-off. And I do find the Internet a pleasant way to buy things.'

Age of criminal responsibility restored to 14

**Law Lords reverse Court of Appeal ruling
lowering limit to 10, but call for law to be reviewed**

Law Lords restored the age of criminal responsibility from 10 back to 14 yesterday, but said the law needed changing.

A Court of Appeal ruling had changed the law a year ago to make ten year-olds as culpable as adults. The law before that – and the position again following the House of Lords judgment yesterday – is that for children aged 10-14 the prosecution has to prove the offenders knew that what they were doing was 'seriously wrong'. The best known cause of this was in 1993, when a jury found that two boys who had murdered the toddler Jamie Bulger had realised the gravity of their crime.

The Home Office last considered – and rejected – reform of the law, which is out of line with most developed countries, in 1990. Last night, Home Office officials said Michael Howard, the Home Secretary, was 'considering' the Lords' judgment.

Five law lords said that, as the law now stood, they had no alternative but to allow an appeal against a High Court decision removing the fundamental legal requirement which has protected generations of children from punishment for criminal actions.

But Lord Lowry, in his leading judgment, said it was time for a much-needed new look at an undoubted problem. 'This is a classic case for parliamentary investigation, deliberation and legislation,' he said.

In the High Court, Lord Justice Mann and Mr Justice Laws had described the rule, highlighted in the Jamie Bulger murder trial, as 'utterly outrageous' and outdated.

By Stephen Ward
Legal Affairs Correspondent

The Law Lords upheld an appeal by a defendant, now 15, against his conviction at the age of 12 for interfering with a motor cycle with intent to commit theft. The boy was fined £60, payable by his mother, who was also bound over to ensure his future good behaviour. The magistrate at Liverpool Youth Court had decided the boy knew that what he was doing was seriously wrong merely because he had run away from the police. The Court of Appeal accepted this was inadequate proof that he had known he was wrong, but then changed the law, so upholding the conviction.

Lord Lowry said the High Court judges had achieved their object in part by drawing renewed attention to serious shortcomings in an important area of criminal law, 'presumption'.

'I believe that the time has come to examine further a doctrine which appears to have been inconsistently applied and which is certainly capable of producing inconsistent results, according to the way in which courts treat the presumption and depending on the evidence to rebut it which is available in each case.'

One solution was to abolish the presumption with or without an increase in the minimum age of criminal responsibility. But that could expose children to the full criminal process at an earlier age than in most western European countries.

An alternative was to give a youth court exclusive jurisdiction – except in family matters – over children up to the age of 14 or 16, applying only civil remedies for anti-social behaviour under 10 or 12 years and both civil and punitive remedies above that age. 'The distinction between the treatment and punishment of child "offenders" has popular and political overtones, a fact which shows that we have been discussing not so much a legal as a social problem, with a dash of politics thrown in, and emphasises that it should be within the exclusive remit of Parliament.'

He said there was a need to study other systems, including that in Scotland, where normal criminal responsibility attaches to a child over eight. Agreeing the appeal should be allowed, Lord Jauncey said it was 'almost an affront to common sense' to presume, for example, that a boy of 12 or 13 who stole a high-powered car, damaged other cars, knocked down a policeman and then ran away was unaware that he was doing wrong.

© *The Independent*
March, 1995

Reversing crime trends

Crime is like a disease, argues Gifty Tawiah, and prevention is better than cure

Almost half of all known offenders are aged under 21 and half of these are under 17. This youth crime is costing Britain £7 billion a year. Crime prevention organisations believe in diverting young people from crime in the first place. If they don't offend, they don't spend their life in and out of prison. This would save money but, more importantly, keeping young people from a life of crime would save them from throwing away their lives. Statistically the biggest proportion of young offenders are male, poor, urban or have come from care. These young people have come from deprived conditions. This deprivation, be it from unemployment or poor social conditions, has been shown to be a factor in criminal behaviour. When people have lots of time to kill and no money to use the time constructively, there is a greater risk that they will not say no when someone offers them the chance of making a quick buck! When you have absolutely nothing – no job, no money, no home – it's easy to start thinking that you are worth nothing and deserve nothing. If you can think this about yourself, then the chances of you not caring much about somebody else, their car (after all they can afford one and you can't) and their home (complete with video and the latest computer games etc.) are greater.

So what is being done to reverse this desperate situation? There has been a lot of media attention about young offenders going on 'holidays' abroad. This has given the impression that social services departments are wasting public money and that young offenders are getting off lightly. The reality is that putting a young person in a young offenders' institution is also very costly and social services departments, rather than being flushed with cash, are starved of staff and resources. The so-called 'holidays abroad' are actually part of a long line of attempts being made by social services and others to turn around the spiral of offending that some young people find themselves in. Places at young offenders' institutions are few and far between and many young offenders often find themselves in adult prisons.

> **Young people are particularly likely to be drawn into vandalism, shop theft and other criminal activity during the long summer holidays, just when they have time on their hands and no money or facilities**

Sadly it's here that they are more likely to learn even more criminal behaviour rather than how not to offend. Humberside Council is asking ten families to take in a young offender from Hull prison (which is only intended for adults but is forced to house young people) because they realise the importance of providing support and not just punishment for young offenders. A spokesman for the council's fostering service said 'The provision of a well-supported community placement could be the difference between them continuing a life of crime and maturing into law-abiding citizens'. Jeremy Bell is the brains behind a project to raise six million pounds to build the SS Renaissance: The first square-rigged commercial sailing ship to be built in Britain for 70 years. Half the crew will be young volunteers at risk of offending. The other half of the crew will be made up of experienced sailors some with experience in teaching in social work. The ship will be carrying aid to the developing world and returning with silk, spices and artefacts.

Jeremy Bell knows this won't be a holiday for the young people. 'The work for those joining the SS Renaissance will be hard, purposeful and in no way a holiday. It will be physically tougher than a boot camp. Without National Service and apprenticeship schemes, there are no rites of passage into adulthood, particularly for young men, and a project like this can fill that need. Any offenders on the programme will be far less likely to offend again. And, those who come from a deprived home will be offered their first real chance in life.'

Young people are particularly likely to be drawn into vandalism, shop theft and other criminal activity during the long summer holidays, just when they have time on their hands and no money or facilities. It is at times like these that work aimed at diverting young people from offending comes into its own. The Splash is a scheme run by many police; Crime Concern and the Southmead Family Project in Bristol offers play schemes and other activities to get young people off the streets and doing something enjoyable, which keeps them out of trouble. As a play scheme worker on the Southmead project says 'ultimately we want to empower the kids so that when they come to make choices about crime and life generally, they think beyond the idea that life is meaningless.'

The above is an extract from the magazine yx, A Daily Express/ Crime Concern Publication.

© yx – Youth Express, Issue 9, Summer Term, 1995

Crime and security

From Help the Aged

One of the most common stories that regularly appears in the press or on television is the one about the elderly man or woman whose life savings have been stolen or who has been viciously attacked by muggers.

Stories such as these are dramatic, disturbing and create the impression that older people are the group in society most at risk from incidents of crime.

While it is certainly the function of the media to report such events, they can also give a distorted picture of crime in the UK. Surprising as it may seem, the 'young' (aged 16-30) are six times more likely than older people to be victims of crime.

Despite these facts, many older people are deeply affected by the reports that they see on television or read about in the press. The 1991 British Gas 'Attitudes to Ageing' survey showed that 45% of people aged 55 or over are worried about becoming a victim of crime, with 13% being 'very worried'.

Many fear being attacked in their own homes and having valued possessions or savings stolen.

This fear of crime can have a very negative effect on people's lifestyle. 'Doris' used to go regularly to dances where she met up with her friends, had a chat and enjoyed an evening out. As a widow, Doris looked forward to her nights out as they provided a welcome change in her daily routine and got her out of her flat.

After learning about an attack on a young woman in her neighbourhood, Doris no longer felt safe enough to go out alone at night. She now only occasionally goes out to dances when she can afford to take a taxi, which isn't very often. The feeling of fear which Doris now has seriously affects the quality of her life and is an experience shared by many older people.

It isn't just the fear of crime on the streets which worries many older people. Many fear being attacked in their own homes and having valued possessions or savings stolen. In recent years, there have been countless reports in the press of older people who have been duped by bogus callers: people posing as a tradesman, for instance, in order to gain entrance to someone's home. It is incidents like these which strike at the very core of people's security and which create a high level of anxiety.

In recent years, groups such as Help the Aged and the Metropolitan Police have launched campaigns to raise public awareness about crime, as a way of reassuring older people and as an opportunity to pass on advice on how they can protect themselves. Help the Aged has also launched a 'Home Safety Campaign' to raise money to provide as many older people as possible with good quality locks, door chains and 'spy-holes' in their doors.

Crime Prevention Officers are now employed at local police stations to give advice on home safety. They

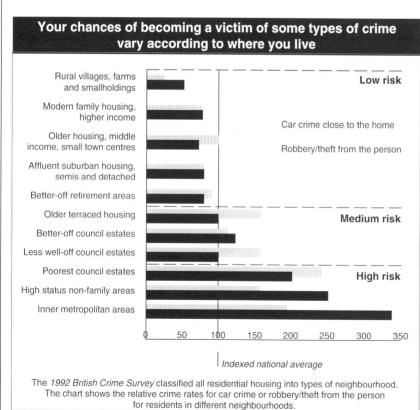

Your chances of becoming a victim of some types of crime vary according to where you live

The *1992 British Crime Survey* classified all residential housing into types of neighbourhood. The chart shows the relative crime rates for car crime or robbery/theft from the person for residents in different neighbourhoods.

Advice to older people

Help the Aged's advice to older people who want to make their homes safer is that they should:

- Keep all windows and doors locked and bolted

- Use a door chain when answering the door

- Check the identity of callers

- If unsure, request a caller to return later

- Keep keys in a safe place

- Cancel milk and regular deliveries before going away on holiday

- Leave some lights on when going out at night.

can advise on the need for security devices and can recommend suitable, reputable installers and fitters. They will also have information about local Neighbourhood Watch Schemes.

Help the Aged stresses that whilst everyone should always take sensible precautions, they should also remember that crime against older people is rare. This is a point the media would do well to reflect in its reports!

© Help the Aged
November 1994

Burglars spurred Keith into action

A series of burglaries spurred a 68 year-old retired man from Leicester into turning the tables on criminals. His efforts won Keith Herbert the first Neighbourhood Watch Medal for central England

He was presented with his Medal and £1,000 by Home Office Minister David Maclean at a special ceremony at the Hyatt Regency in Birmingham.

Keith became involved in Lanesborough Road Neighbourhood Watch three years ago when a burglar tried to break into his house for a second time. He said: 'We were in bed at 12.30am. I had put window locks in, but the raiders had got a spade and were breaking the window. I thought that's enough, I've got to do something about it.'

Since then, everyone in the street has joined the Watch scheme, which covers a quiet residential road close to an inner city area. Over the past two years, burglaries have been cut by two-thirds and in 1994 information from Watch members led to 12 arrests. Keith's quick thinking about a suspicious car led to four arrests, too.

Good communications between Watch members and the police – together with a range of security measures – prove the foundation for this effective scheme. Information sheets and newsletters are supplemented by 'news flashes', word of mouth crime news, mobile links with the local police and intelligence gathering 'walkabouts'. A network of contacts within the ethnic minority community means that the messages reach all residents.

Keith became involved in the Watch movement in 1991 and sounded out the feelings of residents thoroughly before calling a meeting and setting good foundations for a quality scheme.

Keith became co-ordinator and set about identifying the priority areas for action. He set up good links with the police and chivvied the council to improve lighting, cut back hedges and discourage itinerant travellers

from settling on waste land nearby.

He split the Watch area into eight sub-zones of 10 to 12 houses with a contact whose duties include the maintenance of close contact with members and the speedy distribution of communications. Through two teenage members of his contact team and their friends, he has drawn in an enthusiastic and committed group of youngsters.

No members have dropped out of the scheme and meetings are attended in increasing numbers, with well over half of households attending.

Through Keith's efforts, too, 78 households from a multi-ethnic background have been welded into a united and homogenous group.

Together, they are extending their direct crime prevention activities to more indirect measures, involving the whole community in social events and activities.

© Crime Prevention News, June, 1995

21

Your practical guide to crime prevention

Your community

There is a lot you can do outside your home and family to prevent crime. You can take action by getting together with other people and working in partnership with the police to reduce crime in your area. You can help by simply being alert and observant when out and about in your neighbourhood – or you could apply to join the Special Constabulary. Anyone can play some part, however great or small.

Neighbourhood Watch

Neighbourhood Watch schemes are a way for people in an area to get together to help prevent crime and make their neighbourhood a safer place. Neighbourhood Watch is known as Home Watch in some areas, but both work along similar lines and are built on the same idea – of looking after one another and the neighbourhood.

How does it work?

Groups can vary in size, depending on the area and what people want. They target local concerns – like burglary, vandalism or graffiti and devise ways of dealing with them. Individual members decide how active they want to be in the scheme. You could become a committee member or even co-ordinator of a group – or your part could be just keeping an eye on your neighbour's house while they're away.

Schemes develop close links with the police, who can provide advice and information about local problems. Well-run schemes can have a big impact on local crime.

Street Watch

You could also consider joining or setting up a Street Watch scheme – a new idea to use your eyes and ears to help the community. Neighbourhood Watch crime prevention activities are usually centred around people's homes and the immediate surrounding area. Street Watch is a separate scheme to take this a step further. In agreement with local police and local people, members work out specific routes and regularly walk their chosen area.

How does it work?

Street Watch members are ordinary citizens with no police powers. If they spot anything suspicious, all they are asked to do is report it to the police. They can also give active support to vulnerable people by offering transport or escort on foot.

Groups are managed by a co-ordinator who keeps a list of volunteers and provides advice, guidance and support – in consultation with the local police. Street Watch can help reduce crime because members actively use their local knowledge when out and about in their neighbourhood.

Photo: Metropolitan Police

Street Watch guidelines

A set of guidelines for Street Watch activity has been agreed with the police – you can get a copy from your local police station. The guidelines include a basic set of 'Dos and Don'ts', which warn against intervening in an incident. 'Look, listen and report' – but don't 'have a go' and always stay within the law.

Other 'Watch' schemes

Watches need not be confined to residential neighbourhoods. For instance, Business Watches can be very effective in high streets and industrial estates. Farm Watches can encourage farmers to keep an eye on one another's livestock and machinery. Boat Watches can greatly improve the security of marinas and harbours.

Neighbourhood Constables

Neighbourhood Constables are a variation of the existing Special Constables, who are police-trained, uniformed volunteers, with the same powers as a regular officer. Their duties are varied and they can be asked to work anywhere in their police force area.

In contrast, Neighbourhood Constables only work in a specific area – their own neighbourhood, so they become a regular figure on the local scene. In rural areas they may be called Parish Constables, but the idea is the same – to provide more police on the beat, with all the advantages a police presence brings.

Their main duties are foot patrols of a neighbourhood area. Neighbourhood Constables also keep in regular contact with community groups, Neighbourhood Watch and Street schemes, schoolchildren and local traders – promoting initiatives, helping groups and offering advice.

If you want to join
Contact your local police or call 01345 272272 for a Specials Information pack – and note 'Neighbourhood Constable' on your application.

You'll find out more about how to help police reduce crime in your neighbourhood in the booklet *Partners against crime* (see Help! panel and the end of this page).

Crime Prevention Panels
Crime Prevention Panels are locally organised groups who work in partnership with the police to identify local crime problems, and initiate crime prevention measures to deal with them. Panel members are usually local neighbourhood Watch co-ordinators, teachers, local business people or local media representatives. All bring their own particular area of expertise to the work of the panel.

Panel activities are generally related to particular crime problems in the area. Panels will draw up a programme of work, and implement appropriate measures, e.g. fundraising to pay for security devices for elderly people's homes or organising a car window-etching campaign.

Panels can be started by the local police, local business people or community groups (see Help! panel at the end of this page).

Youth Action Groups
These are the young person's version of a crime prevention panel. They are usually attached to a senior panel, or a local school, and deal with areas of crime which are more likely to affect young people such as drug abuse and shoplifting (you can get more advice on youth panels from Crime Concern. See Help! panel at the end of this page).

Voluntary organisations
Many voluntary organisations support and develop crime prevention initiatives in local communities.

● Local Council for Voluntary Service (CVS) – provide advice and support to community groups on a number of issues, including local crime prevention initiatives (see Help! panel).

● Help the Aged and Age Concern – raise funds, educate and administer projects to help provide for the security needs of elderly people.

● NACRO (the National Association for the Care and Resettlement of Offenders) – take on crime problems by involving local residents and agencies on a project basis. NACRO Crime Prevention Unit and the Safe Neighbourhoods Unit offer a range of services to local authorities and other agencies (see Help! panel).

● Crime Concern – an independent national organisation which develops and supports crime prevention initiatives. Works closely with the private sector to produce funding for local projects (see Help! panel).

● Community Action Trust (CAT) – an independent national charity which creates community alliances to fight crime. Crimestoppers, operated by the police seeks anonymous information about crime on a freephone (0800 555 111) with cash rewards available.

Help!
The following publications could be useful:

Neighbourhood watch – a guide to successful schemes – October 1993. Available from Crime Concern, Signal Point, Station Road, Swindon, Wiltshire SN1 1FE Tel: 0179 351 4596.

A practical guide to crime Prevention for local partnership – October 1993.' Available from the Home Office, Crime Prevention Unit, Room 583, 50 Queen Anne's Gate, London SW1H 9AT.

Manual for action – Advice on how to set up a crime prevention panel.

You can get more information on Neighbourhood Watch in the leaflet *Welcome to Neighbourhood Watch*.

The above titles are available from the Home Office, Public Relations Branch, Room 151, 50 Queen Anne's Gate, London SW1H 9AT.

Partners against crime – a guide to helping the police reduce crime in your neighbourhood. Call 0345 235 235 for your free copy.

Local Voluntary Service Councils: for details of your local office, contact the National Association of Councils for Voluntary Service (NACVS), 3rd Floor, Arundel Court, 177 Arundel Street, Sheffield S1 2NU. Tel: 0114 278 6636.

The above is an extract from *Your Practical guide to crime prevention*.

Police reject guns on beat

But most want more officers able to carry arms

By Jason Bennetto
Crime Correspondent

The debate over whether the police should be armed at all times was effectively killed off yesterday when officers voted overwhelmingly against routinely carrying guns. But an equally large number – 83 per cent – called for an increase in the number of officers trained and issued with firearms.

A survey of more than 73,400 officers up to the rank of chief inspector in England and Wales also revealed that officers want greater protection, including access to body armour, while facing increasing threats on their lives.

In the largest police ballot carried out, 79 per cent of rank-and-file officers said they were opposed to being routinely armed. In the Police Federation ballot, the Metropolitan Police had the highest proportion of officers – 35 per cent – in favour of carrying firearms on a daily basis, followed by Greater Manchester (26 per cent), Northumbria (22 per cent), West Yorkshire (22 per cent), and Merseyside (22 per cent).

Just over half the Metropolitan Police officers wanted all men and women in the force to have guns or be trained in their use. There was little difference in the views of young and old officers. But the size of the opposition against routine arming took everyone by surprise.

A small survey last year found that 22 per cent of police constables should be armed on duty. There has been a growing clamour for the police to be routinely armed in response to the greater use of guns by criminals. In the past decade, 19 police officers have been murdered, nine of them in shootings.

> *The size of the opposition against routine arming took everyone by surprise*

In 1993, firearms were used in 4,682 incidents, although against the police in only ten cases. Six officers have been murdered in the past five years.

In the most recent case last month, Constable Philip Walters, 28, who had joined the Metropolitan Police less than two years ago, was shot dead when he and a colleague went to a house in Ilford, East London, after a routine complaint about a disturbance. After the murder Michael Howard, the Home Secretary, said: 'I don't think most police officers in this country want to be armed and I don't think most people in this country want them to be armed.'

Opposition politicians and chief constables have also spoken out against arming on a routine basis. A survey of 1,000 members of the public, also published yesterday, found that only about one in four people supported routine arming, although 63 per cent were in favour of greater availability of guns for officers. Yesterday these sentiments were supported by the police.

Photo: Metropolitan Police

A survey of 1,000 members of the public found that only about one in four people supported routine arming

Gun law: How the police voted

- 74,000 officers took part in the Police Federation poll, the biggest ballot of police opinion ever undertaken.

- 21% said all police should be armed, either on duty or at all times.

- 35% of Metropolitan Police Officers were in favour of being armed.

- 83% were in favour of at least an increase in the number of officers trained and issued with firearms when necessary.

- 11% would refuse to carry a firearm and 6% would resign from the force if ordered to do so.

- 60% said they were dissatisfied with their self-defence training.

But Fred Broughton, chairman of the Police Federation which published the survey on the eve of its annual conference in Bournemouth, denied the vote had quashed any future attempts to introduce routine arming.

He said: 'This result proves, once again, that our police officers acknowledge the vital importance of policing by consent, in partnership with the public, despite the risks they take. At the same time, what has to be acknowledged is that there is huge dissatisfaction with the levels of protection afforded to this country's police officers.'

He added: 'The bobby on the beat faces certain death routinely as we are reminded of that almost on a daily basis.'

The survey, which took in about 60 per cent of officers in England and Wales, also revealed that, in the past two years, more than 52,000 officers had their lives threatened in the cause of duty up to ten times. Up to 55,000 officers were injured by assault between one and ten times in the course of duty in the past two years.

An overwhelming majority of officers were not satisfied with current levels of self-defence training and 90 per cent want cover and overt body armour. Eighty three per cent wanted an increase in the number of officers trained and issued with firearms when necessary. This would involve greater use of specialist armed response vehicles.

The Police Federation yesterday demanded more officers to be trained in the use of firearms, full availability of body armour, better self-defence, and greater willingness to use firearms.

© *The Independent*
May, 1995

Teenage 'narks' may help cops

By Michael Prestage

Police are considering setting up a network of teenage informants – some still at school – who could be paid by officers for providing intelligence on other teenagers.

The idea is backed by Home Secretary Michael Howard, and a 12-month research project will be carried out in Devon and Cornwall into how children and young people can help the police.

With 40 per cent of crime committed by juveniles, the use of teenage informants is viewed as a valuable crime-prevention measure. Currently, however, few police forces use young informants and there are no registered school-age informants.

Det Sgt Sam Balsdon, of Devon and Cornwall Police, who has received a Home Office grant for the study, said: 'It is a subject that is fraught with difficulties, but I believe young informers are a resource that is not being used. No matter how uncomfortable it may seem, people have to accept that young criminals exist and they associate with people their own age.

'If these criminals can be taken out of the system early, and their peers can see they are not benefiting from their crimes, that can only have a good effect.'

Mr Balsdon, who has worked successfully with adult informants since 1977, said many young people would give information without payment if safeguards were given. Anonymity would be guaranteed.

Young people keen to help police would work with officers experienced in handling informants. 'Many youngsters want to fight crime. The message is getting across that they have had enough of those people in their peer group who are destroying their environment and lifestyles. As a police force we rely on this type of attitude.

'The trouble is, at the moment, it is such a grey area. No one is sure what to do with young people who want to pass on information.'

The Government has already recognised informants as a valuable aid to police officers. An Audit Commission report in October 1993 called for greater use of the system, which involves registered individuals being paid by the police for information, but the ethicality of whether to pay children has still to be debated.

© *The Observer*
April, 1995

Spy cameras become part of landscape

Duncan Campbell reports on how use of closed circuit TV is reaching rural areas

Closed circuit television cameras will soon be moving into small towns, villages and residential streets. A huge expansion of the cameras' original role in city shopping centres is already under way.

Applications to the Home Office for funding announced last November by the Home Secretary, Michael Howard, indicate that cameras are due to become as much a part of the British landscape as phone booths and postboxes.

By last Friday, the closing date, more than 200 applications had been received for £2 million of Home Office closed circuit television (CCTV) funding.

The number of CCTV cameras has grown dramatically in the past four years. A survey by the Home Office last year showed that, already, more than 200 schemes in public places were being started, many by commercial interests or under projects like City Challenge or Safer City funding.

A typical example comes from Breckland District Council in Norfolk. It was bid for the maximum £100,000 of funding to place cameras in five towns. The smallest, Swaffham, has a population of 6,000.

One Swaffham resident, freelance photographer Stuart Goodman, says it is a waste of money to install cameras in such a small country place.

Mary Palmer, marketing manager for the council, said that the vast majority of residents favoured the schemes. Property crime in Norfolk had risen by 200 per cent in the past five years, and people were happy if the cameras prevented car break-ins.

Ms Palmer said that schemes already set up in King's Lynn, west Norfolk, had been successful. The first market town to adopt the scheme, King's Lynn, now has more than 60 cameras.

In Notting Hill, west London, police have been leafleting residents for their views on cameras in residential streets. Inspector Alan West, of Notting Hill police, said there could be a case for cameras in areas like Portobello Road where there was street crime, but he first wanted any concerns about cameras to be aired. 'We are not making any assumptions about possible local concerns, and we would do our best to reassure people before any plans were put into place.'

Although there has been little public resistance to the growth of the schemes, the Local Government Information Unit, which has just published a report on CCTV, says that there is a potential for a 'chilling effect' on otherwise legitimate activity, such as a trade union demonstration outside the town hall.

The Government has nailed its flag to the closed circuit television mast. Home Office minister David Maclean calls the camera 'the friendly eye in the sky'. He says: 'There is nothing sinister about it and the innocent have nothing to fear. It will put criminals on the run and the evidence will be clear to see.'

In general, the police back them, too.

But the claims of success have been challenged. Two sociologists, Nic Groombridge, of St Mary's University College, and Karim Murji of Roehampton Institute, who carried out a study for the Institute for the Study and Treatment of Offenders, suggest that around 300,000 security cameras are sold each year and some £300 million is being spent annually on video.

They warn that inflated claims for the success of such schemes are being made by people with an interest in promoting the schemes.

A survey at South Bank University, Southwark, London, last year by Marjorie Bulos and Chris Sarno indicated people felt a 'vague uneasiness about the effect surveillance has on (the) quality of life'. There was some concern from the public about the possibility of CCTV being used 'to spy on people'.

© The Guardian
January, 1995

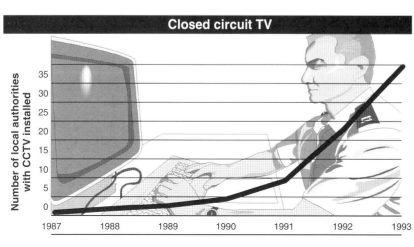

Closed circuit TV

Number of local authorities with CCTV installed (y-axis: 0, 5, 10, 15, 20, 25, 30, 35)

1987 1988 1989 1990 1991 1992 1993

Closed circuit television: future concerns

From *Crime Prevention News*

The growth of Closed Circuit Television is dramatic, and the next few years will see schemes mushrooming in many towns.

At present, about 80 towns and cities have CCTV in their centres and another 150 are deep into the planning stages, with an estimate that around 90 per cent of the boroughs in the UK are considering CCTV.

Furthermore, the recent CCTV funding competition announced by the Home Secretary has attracted well over 450 entries, confirming the continuing surge.

I am a supporter of CCTV and believe that it is a powerful weapon in our fight against crime. Up and down the country I have seen systems which are:

- preventing crime
- deterring criminals
- helping police investigate crime
- helping to convict criminals, and
- reassuring the public.

The quality of the images provided by current equipment is superb and technology has improved in leaps and bounds, with pictures being regularly achieved as good as those provided by our televisions at home.

Current technology can ensure that the inferior images so often seen on Crimewatch and in the press will soon be bad memories.

Unfortunately I have also seen a few poor systems and badly planned and underfunded control rooms, with not enough consideration given to the quality of the operators.

CCTV success lives or dies by the monitoring process, even quality of image is second to that. A system can have the best equipment in the world, but if it is not used properly the effect is wasted.

Philip Edwards
Business Consultant – Home Office Crime Prevention Unit

Civil liberties issues are rarely quoted by the public these days mainly due to the dreadfully sad Bulger case, which was instrumental in convincing the public that 'Big Brother' had now become 'Big Father' and that CCTV was not there to watch them but to watch over them.

However, I see dangers in this rapid expansion. As CCTV works and the 'novelty' wears off, crime may well drop to levels which no longer cause concern.

At this point the focus moves on to another problem area and at this point the already low funding of control rooms may be further reduced. Even now I see systems of over 50 cameras which are being monitored by one operator for up to 12 hours at a time.

Users have become over excited by the technology and are considerably undervaluing the importance of the operators and basic monitoring room operations.

A number of earlier systems are also being trapped into old technology. Their monochrome cameras and monitors with ever-decreasing image quality are gradually becoming obsolete and they are in a Catch 22 situation.

Justification for funding upgrading to modern colour high-tech equipment which produces such vastly superior images cannot be produced on the reduced crime figures.

So equipment will get older and deteriorate further, complacency is likely to set in, and the criminals, quickly realising this, will return to their old haunts.

The other danger is that a system without extremely effective good practice measures will allow illicit tapes to be fed into the public domain by unethical operators. If this is picked up by elements of the press, the public opinion could as easily swing to the other end of the spectrum.

So what are the resolutions?

Those involved in developing and running systems need to:

- ensure that potential users give careful thought and consultation in the pre-planning stages by analysing what problems they wish to resolve
- make CCTV part of a package of measures to resolve the identified problems
- give careful consideration to the aims of the system and how they can be met
- provide quality technical guidance
- ensure systems are staffed with well-trained and reliable personnel on a sensible salary
- develop a definitive Code of Practice
- ensure that funds for upgrading the system over a long term are built into the original budgets and plans
- build in effective and honest evaluation procedures.

If this takes place, CCTV will continue to grow in its effectiveness against crime and the criminals, and the industry's reputation will be enhanced in line with its success, as we make our towns safer places in which to walk, shop and visit.

© *Crime Prevention News*
June, 1995

Imposing the ultimate penalty

Abolished in Britain after a long campaign, the death penalty remains in use in the United States

The death of the British-born man Nicholas Ingram in a Georgia electric chair this month raised mixed emotions about the rights and wrongs of state killings. Ingram was the fifteenth person to be executed in the United States this year. The detailed media coverage of his plight brought into focus the suffering which violent crime causes.

In the 100 years before 1630, 70,000 persons were hanged in England. By 1722 more than 350 capital crimes (offences that carry the death penalty) existed in Britain. Children between 7 and 14 could be hanged for showing 'strong evidence of malice'.

With the wave of social and political reforms (including the extension of voting rights) in the early 19th century, there was a drastic reduction in the use of the death penalty. By 1861 the number of capital crimes had been reduced to four: murder, treason, arson in dock yards and piracy on the high seas.

In the postwar period, there was a series of hangings in which doubt was expressed over the convictions. This public disquiet led to the 1957 Homicide Act. Murder still carried the death penalty, but defences of diminished responsibility and provocation were introduced. In 1962 the hanging of James Hanratty, in what was known as the A6 murder case, fuelled the cause of those seeking to abolish the death penalty. Many believed Hanratty was innocent, and even Janet Gregsen, the widow of his alleged victim, has requested a posthumous pardon.

A national abolition campaign developed, which included organisations such as the Howard League for Penal Reform, church groups and public figures. A Bill abolishing the death penalty was passed in 1965 on a five-year experimental basis. In 1969 abolition was made permanent for all crimes except treason and piracy with violence.

There have been a number of attempts to reintroduce the death penalty since then – often in the aftermath of high-profile murders – but there has always been a majority of opponents in the House of Commons. Abolitionists across the world say the death penalty violates the United Nations Universal Declaration of Human Rights because it denies the right to life and the right not to be tortured or subjected to any cruel, inhuman or degrading punishment.

Opposition to the death penalty in the US is now seen by many as being 'soft' on crime

---

In 1985, the European Convention on Human Rights was extended so that countries could commit themselves to permanent abolition of the death penalty during peacetime. But, in contrast, the US has seen a resurgence in the use of the death penalty. In 1972, following a groundswell of support for abolition accompanying the country's civil rights movement, the Supreme Court ruled that the procedures used in some states were unconstitutional – though capital punishment itself was not – and 600 people awaiting execution had their sentences reduced to life imprisonment. Many states re-wrote their laws in line with the ruling. And in 1976, the Supreme Court found that these new capital punishment laws met constitutional requirements. Over the last 19 years there have been 272 executions; and a further 2,948 people are awaiting execution on death rows across America. Opposition to the death penalty in the US is now seen by many as being 'soft' on crime. In 1992 as Governor of Arkansas, the then presidential hopeful Bill Clinton approved the execution of severely brain-damaged Ricky Ray Rector. Some saw this as a vote-winning exercise. And last

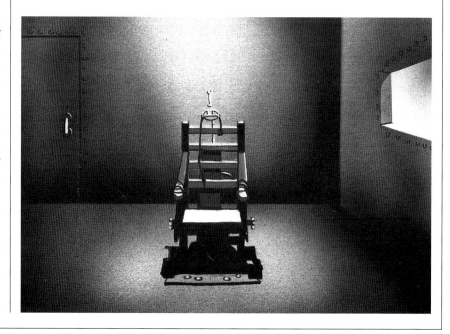

November, Mario Cuomo, the governor of New York state who had opposed capital punishment, was defeated. The state has now reintroduced the death penalty – last used there in 1963 – under the new governor, George E. Pataki. The role of the prosecutor (District Attorney) in the courts of most states is an elected position. Consequently, decisions on whether to call for the death penalty are political, taking account of media coverage and public feeling about each case. The prosecution also has the state's machinery in support, so the scales of justice often appear stacked against the defendant. As Marlene Kamish, lawyer for Manuel Salazar (see box), has stated: 'The relationship between prosecution and defence is one of David and Goliath.'

Over recent years the number of offences qualifying for the death penalty has been increased. In 1988, President Reagan signed the Anti-Drug Abuse Act which created a death penalty offence for certain drug

Manuel Salazar

In 1984, Manuel Salazar was involved in a struggle with a police officer in Illinois. Salazar was severely beaten, but the policeman was killed. Salazar, of Hispanic origin, was tried by an all-white jury, found guilty and sentenced to death. While on death row, Salazar, who claims the killing was in self-defence, began to paint. An international campaign, including a travelling exhibition of his work, helped highlight his case. Last September, the Illinois Supreme Court decided to grant him a retrial.

trafficking activities. And last year President Clinton introduced the death penalty for more than 50 offences under the Federal Death Penalty Act. This legislation made the death penalty applicable for several offences where there was no loss of life – such as the attempted assassination of the President, treason and espionage. But the US is not alone. China executes more than 2,500 people each year with 60 crimes – among them hooliganism – carrying the death penalty. Beheading is the manner of execution in Saudi Arabia, with confessions extracted under torture proving sufficient evidence for a conviction. The world-wide trend, however, is against capital punishment, with Italy becoming the latest country to abolish the death penalty last year. Among the most outspoken opponents of capital punishment in the US is the former Justice of the Supreme Court, Harry A. Blackmun. He has stated that the death penalty as administered in the US is unconstitutional and 'remains fraught with arbitrariness, discrimination, caprice (vindictiveness) and mistakes'.

© The Guardian
April, 1995

The death penalty across the United States

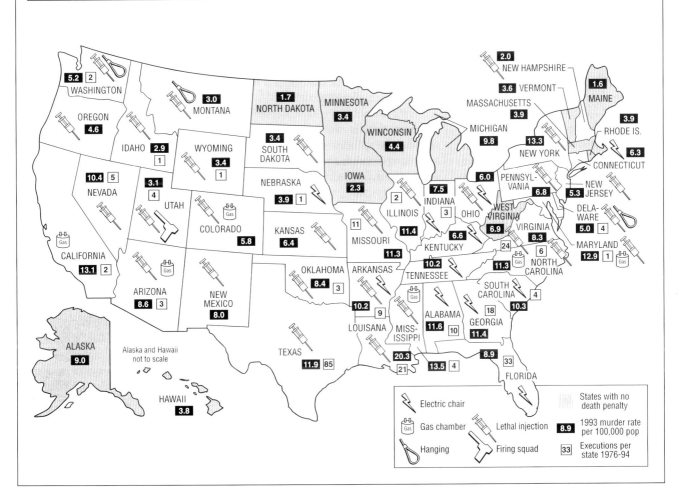

A sanction fit for murderers

By Gary L. McDowell

The political controversy that has surrounded the death penalty in the United States for the past quarter of a century has reached Britain. The efforts of Nicholas Ingram's attorney to have Georgia's law governing capital punishment declared unconstitutional has inevitably drawn public attention to the deeper question of its morality.

The undercurrent of criticism has been that the ultimate sanction is indeed immoral, even if constitutional in the eyes of the US Supreme Court. Moreover, there seems to be a confidence that only a morally deficient country could contemplate putting to death even those who commit such heinous crimes as that for which Ingram was properly convicted.

That view is simply wrong: there is a moral foundation for capital punishment, and it is one that must be defended if liberal democracies are to survive.

At least since Aristotle wrote, there has been an understanding that politics and morality are inextricably linked. By their nature, men reason about what is right and wrong, collectively deliberate about it, and make political judgements in the form of laws. To serve its function, law must carry a sanction that will reflect the moral seriousness of the offence.

Modern constitutionalism, of which the US constitution remains the exemplar, took its bearings from such English writers as Thomas Hobbes and John Locke. For them, man was born in a state of nature, where no law obtained and where, as a result, as Hobbes so memorably put it, life was 'solitary, poor, nasty, brutish and short'. The solution to that barbaric and primitive state was the social contract whereby men would cede certain of their natural rights to enter into a civil society.

What distinguished this civil order was law; and it was by law that men would know with certainty what was just and unjust.

There is a moral foundation for capital punishment, and it is one that must be defended

The defining characteristic of modern constitutionalism is a faith in governmental structures whereby the moral sense of the people is given vent. Through public deliberation, notions of right and wrong do battle until a general consensus emerges; thus are private opinions about justice transformed into something approximating the public good in the form of legally binding rules.

For the rules to be obeyed, they must be accompanied by a sanction that fits the crime. There is no crime more antithetical to the idea of a civil society of free individuals than murder. It is therefore altogether fitting that the people in their collective moral capacity should decree that those who deliberately take a life shall pay with their own. It is a legitimate expression of moral indignation, a notice that certain acts are simply unacceptable and that those who commit them will forfeit their right to participate in civil society. Life imprisonment is insufficient.

That is not barbarism; that is not moral deficiency; that is the rule of law. It is the moral peg on which everyone's freedom ultimately hangs.

● The writer is Director of the Institute of United States Studies and Professor of American Studies in the University of London.

© The Independent
April, 1995

Photo: Mike Grieve

For the rules to be obeyed, they must be accompanied by a sanction that fits the crime

'Let him fry,'
say folks of Georgia

Nicholas Ingram awaits execution in Jackson, Georgia

Nicholas Ingham may be acquiring something of a martyr's status in the Britain he left as a year-old infant. But here in rural Georgia scarcely a person does not approve of his scheduled execution tonight – and the way it will be carried out.

'I think it's right. Criminals should know that, if they are found guilty of murdering someone, they are going to die,' said Megan, a 19-year-old caller to Atlanta's WSG talk radio show.

And half a dozen others made the same point. Indeed, until the British media took up his case, Nicholas Ingram was anything but a celebrity in the US.

Even as his last appeals tick away, the story still rates just a few paragraphs on the inside pages of the Atlanta press, in which the issue is not capital punishment but how for convicts like Ingram 12 years can elapse between sentencing and execution – assuming it takes place tonight. The media in America beyond have barely noticed it.

Capital punishment is as old as Georgia, and the deep South is its special province. The state has put 18 people to death since executions resumed here in 1983. 'Turn on the juice, fry him, and don't let's hear his name again,' said WSG host Neil Bortz, self-proclaimed 'mouth of the South'.

Polls show 90 per cent of Georgians agree. The main point of controversy for Bortz's listeners was whether Georgia's electricity utility was refusing to provide the power for the execution, forcing the prison to rely on its own generator. The electric chair itself causes no special revulsion: 'If they're gonna die, they're gonna die.'

From Rupert Cornwell in Jackson, Georgia

The only dissenting voice was the *Atlanta Constitution*, which acknowledged what is conveniently forgotten here, that the death penalty is no deterrent and Britain's murder rate is 14 times less than America's. Noting the outcry in the US last year when 18 year-old Michael Fay was caned in Singapore, it wrote: 'There is a reason this country doesn't cane vandals, cut off the hands of those who steal, or castrate those who rape. It's called civilisation.'

© *The Independent*
April, 1995

Waiting to die

The last hour
- Guarded by four warders, Ingram goes to reception room by death chamber to say farewell to loved ones.
- Chaplain accompanies him to chamber for final prayers.
- Up to 12 witnesses take their place in adjoining viewing room.

In the chamber
- Electric chair made of solid oak 51 years ago. Polished weekly by death row prisoners.
- Electric cable, 1 inch in diameter, snakes across floor into chair's base.
- Small pans of salt water, which facilitate better electrical contact, placed near back of chair.
- Ten thick leather straps with heavy iron buckles secure Ingram into chair.
- Death cap – a metal plate which carries the charge to the shaven skull – is fixed by strap under chin.
- Hood, an oblong piece of leather stretching from above his ears to below his chest, is fixed to his head.

The execution
- In a second viewing room, three guards stand beside three buttons. No one knows which one triggers charge. A supervisor waits by phone for possible reprieve.
- When button is pressed, 2,400 volts surge into the body in two minute bursts. Doctors wait ten minutes for body to cool before examination. If still alive, another two-minute burst administered. Final cause of death is usually heart failure.

© *Daily Mail*
April, 1995

Death penalty

By Amnesty International

Amnesty International opposes the death penalty in every country and under any circumstances. Amnesty believes that:

- the death penalty is a violation of the right to life and the right not to be subjected to cruel, unusual or degrading punishment, as proclaimed in the Universal Declaration of Human Rights.

- the death penalty does not serve as a deterrent to murder and crime.

- the death penalty is disproportionately imposed upon the poor, on racial minorities, on the mentally ill and on those without adequate legal counsel.

- the death penalty kills innocent people.

During 1994, 2,331 prisoners are known to have been executed in 37 countries, and 4,032 sentenced to death in 75 countries. These figures include only cases known to Amnesty International. The true figures are certainly higher.

Despite these alarming figures, the trend worldwide is towards abolition. As of January 1995, 54 countries had abolished the death penalty for all crimes, 15 had abolished it for all but exceptional crimes such as wartime crimes, and 27 countries and territories were abolitionist *de facto* in that, while retaining the death penalty in law, they have not executed anyone for at least 10 years. Ninety-seven countries retain and use the death penalty. Nearly half of all countries are now abolitionist in either law or practice.

A small number of countries account for the vast majority of executions recorded. Amnesty International received reports of 1,791 executions in China, 139 executions in Iran and over 100 in Nigeria. These three countries alone accounted for 87% of all executions recorded by Amnesty International worldwide in 1994. Amnesty also received reports of several hundred executions in Iraq but was unable to confirm most of these reports or to give an exact figure.

Japan

Until recently, Japan appeared to be following the worldwide trend towards abolition, having carried out no executions between late 1989 and 1993. This trend now appears to be changing. Nine people have been executed since 1993 and there are currently over 90 people on death row in Japan, 57 of them having exhausted all of their appeals.

Ninety-seven countries retain and use the death penalty

Prisoners have been selected for execution on an arbitrary basis. The prevailing political situation and the personal beliefs of the individual Minister of Justice appear to exert undue influence on the decision to order the execution. Amnesty has received reports that prisoners have been denied access to lawyers and have been forced to sign false confessions. In addition, it is extremely difficult for a prisoner to obtain a retrial once the sentence has been finalised. Amnesty International is concerned that many prisoners have been denied the possibility of retrial even though their lawyers have put forward reports which suggest that the original trials were unfair.

United States of America

The new state governor of New York, George E. Pataki, has announced his support for reinstating the death penalty. Should the death penalty be reintroduced in New York, the state will become one of an increasing number of states returning to the use of executions. Since 1991, seven states have resumed executions.

Governor Pataki cites strong public support for his proposals and this, in part, apparently justifies the death penalty's reintroduction. This argument is misleading and simplistic. A poll which asks, 'Do you support the death penalty?' will result in a strong 'yes'. However, when presented with alternatives to capital punishment and with evidence refuting the reliability of the deterrence argument (see opposite), the results are very different. In 1991, a survey presented New Yorkers with a range of possible sanctions in addition to the death penalty. A vast majority (73% to 19%) favoured life without parole coupled with restitution to the victim's family over the death penalty.

Since the use of the death penalty was resumed in the United States in the mid-1970s, 258 executions have been carried out. Nine juvenile offenders have been executed since 1977 and at least 13 juvenile offenders remain on death row in 13 states. As of October 1994, 40.3% of those on death row were black and yet black people make up only 12.6% of the total US population. Those accused of homicide involving white victims are far more likely to receive a death sentence than those convicted of killing black people. In 1994 US Supreme Court Justice, Harry A. Blackmun declared:

I feel morally and intellectually obligated simply to concede that the death penalty experiment has failed. He added that the death penalty remains fraught with arbitrariness, discrimination, caprice and mistake

Pakistan

The case of Salamat Masih, a Christian juvenile sentenced to death on 9 February 1995 for blasphemy and acquitted two weeks later by the Lahore High Court, made people around the world aware that Pakistan is one of the few countries that still uses the death penalty against juveniles. Had the death penalty been carried out, Salamat Masih would have been the second juvenile executed in Pakistan since 1990.

The United Nations Convention on the Rights of the Child asserts that the death penalty may not be imposed on anyone below the age of 18 at the time of the offence. Pakistan was a party to this Convention. There is a growing consensus that the execution of juveniles is contrary to international law. The only other countries known to have executed juveniles since 1990 are the United States, Yemen and Saudi Arabia.

A form of deterrence?

The argument most frequently used for the death penalty is deterrence. The deterrence argument states that it is necessary to kill an offender to dissuade other people from committing the same kind of crime. Empirical evidence does not support this argument. It is incorrect to assume that all, or most, of those who commit such serious crimes as murder do so after rationally calculating the consequences. Murders are most often committed in moments of passion, when extreme emotion overcomes reason. They may also be committed under the influence of alcohol or drugs, or in moments of panic, for example, when the perpetrator is caught in the act of stealing. Some people who commit violent crime are highly unstable or mentally ill. In none of these cases can fear of the death penalty be expected to deter. The deterrence argument is not borne out by the facts. If the death penalty did deter potential offenders more effectively than other punishments, one would expect to find that those countries or jurisdictions which have the death penalty for a particular crime would have a lower rate of crime than those which do not. Similarly, a rise in the rate of crimes hitherto punishable by death would be expected in states which abolish the penalty, and a decline in crime rates would be expected among states which introduce the death penalty for those crimes. Yet study after study has failed to establish any such link between the death penalty and crime rates.

Murders are most often committed in moments of passion, when extreme emotion overcomes reason

---

Perhaps the opposite may even be argued: that the death penalty may in fact increase crime rates. For example, in the United States this may have been the case. In the three years following the resumption of executions, the state of Florida (1980-82) had the highest murder rates in the state's recent history, with a 28 per cent increase in homicides in 1980. Although the homicide rate fell in 1982 and 1983, it remained higher than the period immediately before 1979, and rose again slightly in 1984.

The way we have carried out executions historically in the United States appears to have contributed slightly but significantly to the increase in homicides.
William J. Bowers and Glenn L. Pierce, Criminologists, USA

In Georgia, where executions resumed in 1983, the homicide rate increased by 20 per cent in 1984, a year in which the national homicide rate fell by 5 per cent.

History of the death penalty in the UK

The Murder (Abolition of Death Penalty) Act, in 1965 abolished death penalty for murder for a five-year experimental period. Abolition of the death penalty for murder in Great Britain was made permanent by resolutions of both Houses of Parliament on 18 December 1969. However, the death penalty is retained for high treason both in peacetime and in wartime under the Treason Act, 1914, and in England and Wales for piracy with violence under the Piracy Act, 1837. The Army Act of 1955 and the Naval Discipline Act of 1981, retain the death penalty for a number of offences committed by members of the armed forces during wartime. A death penalty may not be imposed on anyone who was aged under 18 at the time of the offence, nor on a woman pregnant at the date of the imposition of the sentence. The last executions – of two men convicted of murder – were on 13 August 1964.

A move to reintroduce the death penalty for common crimes was defeated in the House of Commons of the United Kingdom on 17 December 1990 by 367 votes to 182 – a margin of 185 votes larger than in 1988 when a similar motion was rejected.

About the death penalty

Assassination on the scaffold is the worst form of assassination because there it is invested with the approval of society… Criminals do not die by the hands of the law. They die by the hands of other men.

George Bernard Shaw, 1903

Murderer is man plus murder. Real justice is done when the judge punishes the murder and restores the man.

Former Justice V. R. Krishna Iyer, Supreme Court of India

My primary concern here is not compassion for the murderer. My concern is for the society which adopts vengeance as an acceptable motive for its collective behaviour. If we make that choice, we will snuff out some of that boundless hope and confidence in ourselves and other people, which has marked our maturing as a free people.

Pierre Elliott Trudeau, Former Prime Minister of Canada.

The fruit of my experience has this bitter after-taste: that I do not believe that any one of the hundreds of executions I carried out has in any way acted as a deterrent against future murder. Capital punishment in my view achieved nothing except revenge.

Albert Pierrepoint, Britain's Hangman for 25 years

The one who pursues revenge should dig two graves. (Chinese proverb)

© Amnesty International

INDEX

ADDITIONAL RESOURCES

You might like to contact the following organisations for further information. Due to the increasing cost of postage, many organisations cannot respond to inquiries unless they receive a stamped, addressed envelope.

Amnesty International – British Section
99-119 Roseberry Avenue
London EC1R 4RE
Tel: 0171 814 6200

Publishes a pack on capital punishment.

Apex Trust
2-4 Colchester Street
London E1 7TG
Tel: 0171 481 4831
Fax: 0171 481 8584

Objects are to improve the job prospects of those who have a criminal record, as employment is a major factor in achieving rehabilitation and reducing the risk of re-offending.

Black Female Prisoners Scheme
Brixton Enterprise Centre
444 Brixton Road
London SW9 8EJ
Tel: 0171 733 5520

Provides a service re-introducing the offender back into the community.

Crime Concern
Signal Point
Station Road
Swindon
Wiltshire
SN1 1FE
Tel: 01793 514 596

INQUEST
Ground Floor
Alexandra National House
330 Seven Sisters Road
London N4 2PJ
Tel: 0181 802 7430
Fax: 0181 801 7450

Supports people who are trying to obtain justice through the coroner's inquest system. To campaign against deaths in custody and on related issues and for changes in coroner's procedures.

Institute for the Study and Treatment of Delinquency
King's College London
Chelsea Campus
Manresa Road
London SW3 6LX
Tel: 0171 333 4890
Fax: 0171 333 4888

Promotes the exchange of knowledge and experience of criminal justice matters among all interested people, both professional and lay.

JUSTICE
95a Chancery Lane
London WC2A 1DT
Tel: 0171 405 6018
Fax: 0171 831 1155

Objects are to uphold and strengthen the principles of the rule of law in territories for which the British parliament is directly or ultimately responsible.

Legal Action for Women (LAW)
Kings Cross Women's Centre
71 Tonbridge Street
London WC1H 9DZ
Tel: 0171 837 7509

Runs a grassroots service for all women where legal problems are dealt with as part of women's whole lives.

Metropolitan Police
New Scotland Yard
Broadway
London
SW1H 0BG
Tel: 0171 2302434

NCH Action for Children
85 Highbury Park
London N5 1UD
Tel: 0171 226 2033
Fax: 0171 226 2537
Runs family and community centres nationwide for children and families who are victims of domestic violence.

Peace Ethics Animals and Consistant Human Rights (PEACH)
88 Cobden Street
Luton
Beds LU2 0NG
Tel: 01582 459943

Opposes violations of the right to life by war, the death penalty, abortion, eugenics and poverty.

Prison Reform Trust
The Old Trading House
2nd Floor
15 Northburgh Street
London EC1V 0AH
Tel: 0171 251 5070

Publishes a wide range of publications including *A Look Inside*, a response pack about prisons. Ask for their publications list.

Prisoners Reform Trust
59 Caledonian Road
London N1 9BU
Tel: 0171 251 5070
Fax: 0171 833 5543

Promotes public understanding of the need for improvements in our prison system.

The Howard League for Penal Reform
708 Holloway Road
London N19 3NL
Tel: 0171 2817722
Fax: 0171 281 5506

To provide facilities for education, research and critical analysis of the criminal justice and penal system in the UK and Europe. Publish a wide range of useful factsheets.

Women in Prison
22 Highbury Grove
London N5 2EA
Tel: 0171 226 5879

Campaigns for the welfare and support of women in prison.

ACKNOWLEDGEMENTS

The publisher is grateful for permission to reproduce the following material.

Chapter One: Crime

Killings rise as Britain becomes more violent, © The Independent, April 1995, *Car and property crime falls as violence rises,* © The Guardian, April 1995, *Children and crime,* © The Howard League for Penal Reform, 1994, *From vandals in Newcastle to louts in Guildford,* © The Guardian, September 1994, *A boy's view of right and wrong,* © The Independent, March 1995, *Experts call for a system to deal with young offenders,* © The Independent, March 1995, *Youth culture linked to rise in delinquency,* © The Independent, May 1995, *From the cradle to criminality,* © The Times, February 1995, *Scientist denounces criminal gene theory,* © The Independent, February 1995, *Companies beware: computer crime can dent your profits,* © Crime Prevention News, December 1994, *Crime gangs use Internet to access credit card fraud,* © The Independent, June 1995, *Children taught crime on internet,* © The Telegraph Plc, London 1995, *Chilli order led to a £1,000 sting,* © The Independent, June 1995, *Age of criminal responsibility restored to 14,* © The Independent, March 1995, *Reversing crime trends,* © yx, Issue 9, Summer Term 1995.

Chapter Two: Crime Prevention

Crime and security, © Help the Aged, November 1994, *Burglars spurred Keith into action,* © Crime Prevention News, June 1995, *Your practical guide to crime prevention,* © HMSO Reproduced with the Kind Permission of Her Majesty's Stationery Office, 1995, *Police reject guns on beat,* © The Independent, May 1995, *Teenage 'narks' may help cops,* © The Observer, April 1995, *Spy cameras become part of landscape,* © The Guardian, January 1995, *Closed circuit television: future concerns,* © Crime Prevention News, June 1995, *Cracking crime by keyboard,* © Crime Prevention News, March 1995, *Second try for tagging,* © Legal Action, February 1995.

Chapter Three: Capital Punishment

Should we kill the killers?, © The Guardian, April 1995, *Imposing the ultimate penalty,* © The Guardian, April 1995, *The cruelty of execution,* © The Howard League for Penal Reform, *European body calls for anti-death penalty,* © Council of Europe, March 1994, *A sanction fit for murderers,* © The Independent, April 1995, *'Let him fry,' say folks of Georgia,* © The Independent, April 1995, *Death penalty,* © Amnesty International.

Photographs and Illustrations

Pages 1, 30: Anthony Haythornthwaite/Folio Collective, page 6: Emma Dodd/Folio Collective, pages 8, 15, 23: Andrew Smith/Folio Collective, page 9: Ulrike Preuss/Format, pages 11, 12: Ken Pyne, pages 22, 24: Metropolitan Police, page 34: Mike Grieve.

Craig Donnellan
Cambridge
September, 1995